Nature's Paradise

Edited by Donna Samworth

forwardpress

First published in Great Britain in 2008 by:
Forward Press Ltd.
Remus House
Coltsfoot Drive
Peterborough
PE2 9JX
Telephone: 01733 898101
Website: www.forwardpress.co.uk

SB ISBN 978-1 84602 066 7

Foreword

Although we are a nation of poets we are accused of not reading poetry, or buying poetry books. After many years of listening to the incessant gripes of poetry publishers, I can only assume that the books they publish, in general, are books that most people do not want to read.

Poetry should not be obscure, introverted, and as cryptic as a crossword puzzle: it is the poet's duty to reach out and embrace the world.

The world owes the poet nothing and we should not be expected to dig and delve into a rambling discourse searching for some inner meaning.

The reason we write poetry (and almost all of us do) is because we want to communicate: an ideal; an idea; or a specific feeling. Poetry is as essential in communication, as a letter; a radio; a telephone, and the main criterion for selecting the poems in this anthology is very simple: they communicate.

Contents

Summer's All	Clive Cornwall	1
Once Summer's Gone	Susan Mullinger	1
Capricorn Moon	Ben Macnair	2
First Summer	Karen Wood	3
Weather Wise	William Stannard	4
Ever Wondered?	Marvyn Attwell	5
City	Clare Todd	5
The Millennium Year	Eunice Ogunkoya	6
Summer In The Garden	Rosalind Ann Webb	6
Days In Mijas	Rosemary Keith	7
Purification	Anthony John Ward	8
Angel In A Cloud	Jacqueline Claire Davies	9
Summer Symbols	Muhammad Khurram Salim	9
A Wayward Child Of Mother Earth	Mark Marsh	10
Seashore	Joan Elizabeth Blissett	11
The Crying Seasons	Victorine Lejeune-Stubbs	12
Earth's Love	S A Brown	12
A Summer Day	Joan Hosker	13
Yarmouth Beach	Adrian Bullard	13
Elysian Fields	Kristen Wood & Adam Poole	14
Games People Play	Warren Fraser	14
Secret Summer	Sue Wilson	15
Small Pleasures	Maureen Arnold	15
Summer Sensations	Brenda Hughes	16
Summer Visitor	Muriel Nicola Waldt	16
View From The Low Path	Miki Byrne	17
Summer Fun	Julie Marie Laura Shearing	17
Sunny	Stella Bush-Payne	18
A Summer's Tale, Stratford-Upon-Avon	Carole Luke	19
Butterfly Ridge	Ernest Hannam	20
That Sunny Day	Mary Hughes	21
Holidays	Gordon Andrews	22
Visions	Linda Wilson	22
Speculation	Rosaleen Clarke	23
June 21st	Norman Bissett	23
Away With The Fairies	Kath Cooley	24
Tree Leaves	Bav	24
School Holidays	Chris Leith	25

Last Summer - Haiku	Johana West	25
Endless Summers	Ray Fenech	26
July	Joyce Walker	27
Summer Isn't Over Yet	Sarah Louise Dermody	28
Summer Secrets	Finnan Boyle	28
Summer	Annabelle Tipper	29
Whispering	Carole A Cleverdon	29
A Summer Storm	Celia G Thomas	30
Summer Skies	Agnes Hickling	31
Castaway	Heather Pickering	32
Vagary Vacation	John Waby	33
Summer Chats	Carolie Cole Pemberton	34
Barcarolle	Margaret Bennett	34
In British Summertime	Matt Doran	35
Sonnet: I Remem'er	Jasmine Kang	35
Tree Time	Richard Lyes	36
Daddy Bunchie	Dranoel Yengid	36
Emma's Cottage	Karen Zena Roberts	37
Crowhurst	Peter Alfred Buss	37
Lunar Promise	David Reddall	38
A Summer Shower	Christine Hardemon	38
The Treasures Of Darkness	Beryl Moorehead	39
Summer	D McDonald	39
Childhood	Sheena Blackhall	40
The Beach	Carol Paxton	40
Summer Chameleon	Ali Sebastian	41
Seasonal Touch	Lorna Tippett	42
Vista Views	Roger Thornton	42
Summer	David Sheasby	43
Fun In The Sun	Christopher Head	43
Summer Expectations	Joyce Hockley	44
August 2007	Steve Glason	45
Darkness Descends on Upton-Upon-Severn	Guy Fletcher	46
Dancing Snowflakes	Meryl Champion	46
Storm Brewing	Barnabas Tiburtius	47
Summer Sensations	Tom Cabin	47
The Sun	Daphne Fryer	48
Forever Summer	Isabel Cortan	48
Waiting For A Lecture	Debra Ayis	49
Lost Spirit	Joan Hammond	49
Settle In Seattle	Philip John Loudon	50

Stirred Memories	Bryan Clarke	51
The Farm	Joan Woolley	52
Summer Storm	David Lin	53
Dream Away A Summer's Day	Catherine Mary Armstrong	54
Picturesque	Beverly Maiden	54
Gemini Bay	Stephen Paul Sunter	55
Summer Is On Its Way	Colin Hush	55
Seaside	Shirley Brooks	56
Holiday	Royston Herbert	57
Summer Floods	Paul Byron Norris	58
Summer Reflections	Arthur Pickles	58
Whispering Wind	Debbie Storey	59
The Sun	Nicola Barnes	59
English Summer	David Garde	60
My Old Friend	Fiona Cary	61
Sniping At Summer	Di Bagshawe	62
The Painter	Lorna Lea	63
Tunisian Sunsets	Margaret Pedley	64
The Sea	John Cook	64
Summer Memories	Christine Naylor	65
On The Beach	Stanley Downing	65
Idyllic Imminence	Annie Harcus	66
Suffolk Summer (A Kyrielle)	Peter Davies	67
Summer	Lynda Hughes	67
My Special Moment	Barbara Jermyn	68
Black Money	David Charles	69
Holiday Shangri-La	Pauline Jones	70
Summer Fête	Len Peach	72
The Sun-Worshippers	John Green	73
Summer Oasis	George Carrick	74
The Seaside	Cathy Mearman	74
Summer On The Beach	Alasdair Sclater	75
Early Summer	Mary Tickle	75
Summer Reflections	Brian Wood	76
Sunny Honey	Jagdeesh Sokhal	76
To A Newt	Ian Burnett	77
Floods	Richard Trowbridge	78
Spring	Sybille Krivenko	78
Summer Magic	Kathleen Mary Scatchard	79
My Garden In May	Rachel Van Den Bergen	79
San Gimignano	Maggie Andrews	80
Heatwave	Rosemary Benzing	81

Untitled	Tomboy	82
Wet, Wet, Wet Wetland . . .	Chris Creedon	83
Diamanté; A South American Dream	Ann Hubbard	84
Enchanting Butterfly	Joanna Maria John	84
This Summer	Linda Hurdwell	85
The Violent Storm	PB James	85
It's The Summertime Once Again	Samantha Rose Whitworth	86
Nature's Patterns	Valma June Streatfield	87
The Hot Nevada Sun	Rod Trott	88
In The Spring	A V Carlin	88
The Lonely Duck	Dorothy Foster	89
Bluebell Wood At Brockweir	Eileen M Lodge	89
Summer Days	Olive Young	90
The Fish	Teresa Webster	91
Enchanted	Jane Cooter	92
Summer Days	Terry Powell	93
Other Worlds - Other Lives	Sue Cann	94
Where Peace And Love Abides	Maureen Westwood O'Hara	95
Wild-Fowlers Call The Fens Their Own	Gillian Fisher	96
Skyline	Melissa Brabanski	96
Adventurers' Fen	Anita Richards	97
God Of All Creation	Wendy Calow	97
Spring's Glory	Gordon Forbes	98
Sunrise	Trevor De Luca	98
The Floods; Summer 2007	Catherine Blackett	99
Springtime On Shipbourne Common	Betty Willeard	99
All For Free	Gloria Hargreaves	100
Buttercups And Daisies	Mick Nash	101
Come Spring	Linda Coleman	102
The Coming Of Winter	Olive White	103
Summer's Flight	Maureen Plenderleith	104
Springtime	Donna Salisbury	104
My Golden Champa Tree	Rumjhum Biswas	105
Spring Has Sprung	Claire Rushbrook	106
Down In Our Wood	Sheila High	107
Haute Marne	Christina Stowell	108
Spring	Jean Martin-Doyle	108
A Delightful Cycle Ride	Anne Churchward	109

Springtime	Vera Hankins	109
To English Hills Baptised In Eden	David Walford	110
Crystal Morn	Ann-Marie Williamson	111
As Sunset Dims	Marian Theodora Maddison	112
Came The Day	John Clarke	112
I Choose Nature As My Bride	Bolaji St Ramos	113
New Life	Joan M Waller	113
A Bright Jewel	Valerie Hall	114
Nature's Power	LAG Butler	114
The Hard Outer Layer	H J Clark	115
Plant	Barry Bradshaigh	115
Walking With Trees	Ivy Allpress	116
Gardens	Rizwan Akhtar	116
Observe And Ponder	Stacey Morgan	117
Nature's Wonder	Terri Brant	117
April Blossoming	James Stephen Cameron	118
Mother's Nature	Paulette Francesca Sedgwick	119
The Highlands	G Morrison	120
A Dragonfly	Edmund Saint George Mooney	120
Grey Sky In Summer	Margaret Miles	121
The Soul Of The Waters	Mariana Zavati Gardner	121
A Recipe For Spring	Joanne Hale	122
Spring Will Be A Little Early This Year	Joanna Wallfisch	124
A Storm Is Coming	Joanne Starkie	125
Return Of Spring	Doreen Kowalska	126
Springtime	Janet Cavill	127
Springtime	Margaret Worsley	128
Frosty Night	Joan Kniveton	128
Urban Or Landscape	B W Ballard	129
Birth Of A Season	William Adam	130
Spring	S J Sanders	130
Ode To Pollen	Lila Joseph	131
Bluebells	Joyce Hudspith	131
Morello Cherry Blossom	Mary Pauline Winter (nee Coleman)	132
Sprouted Spring This Season	Soma Das	133
Sunshine And Showers	M L Damsell	134
Remembering	Doreen Williams	135
Lent	Edgar Wyatt Stephens	136
Spring	Nancy Solly	137

A Place Called Vrnwy	J Barker	138
Autumn Month	Jean McGovern	139
Springtime	Margaret Burtenshaw-Haines	140
Just Round The Corner	E D Bowen	140
On A Storm	Stephen Tuffnell	141
April In Lincolnshire	Derek Webster	142
Orchid	Denise Delaney	143
The First Spring	John Eccles	144
Unfaithful Friends	Margaret Wilson	145
Spring Is Here	Beth Izatt Anderson	146
The Escape Of Spring	Margaret Ballard	147
In The Bosom Of Creation	Patrick L Glasson	148
A Field Into Harvest	Maureen Thornton	149
Take A Walk On The Wild Side	Charles Keeble	150
It's Nature	D J Wooding	151
Sonnets For Late Spring	Robert D Hayward	152
Mother Nature	Abder R Derradji	153
Spring	Colin T C Mercer	154
Spring In Your Step	Julie Ashpool	155
A Lovely Garden	Zoe French	156
Changing Seasons	V N King	157
The Colt	Catherine Armstrong	158
Red Grass	Richard Stead	159
Awakening	A Quinn	160
On Golden Pond	R H Sunshine	160
Wonderful Nature	Joan Igesund	161
The Tree	George Coombs	161
Sudden Spring	Barrie Williams	162
Moonstruck	Ann Wardlaw	163
Cherry Blossom	Gillian Jones	164
Waltz Of The Willows	Frances Gibson	164
Autumn	N Evans	165
Love And Nature	Eileen Finlinson	165
The Changing Seasons	Marilyn Hine	166
Lingering	Pauletta Edwards	167
A Song Frozen In Time	Margaret Webster	168
The Beauty Of Our Earth	D N Wright	169
Nature's Beauty	S Meredith	170
Sossusvlei	Iris Ina Glatz	171
Legacy	Babsi Sherwin	172
Soon I Will Be Leaving	Don Woods	173
My Bonnie Teviotdale	Elizabeth Murray Shipley	174

Heron	Lilian Perriman	174
The Boat Ride	Stephen Shutak	175
Beyond The Horizon	Margaret Parnell	176
Nature's Choice	Gareth Culshaw	177
Pine Cone	Christian Hinz & Shelley Powell	177
A Favourite Walk	June Melbourn	178
Controversy Over Weather	Hazel Palmer	179
The Water Element	Eunice Ogunkoya	180
The Fenland Revisited	Raymond W Seaton	181
A Change Is Required	Ron Martin	182
Bluebell Woods	Terry Daley	183
Nature	Betty Prescott	184
The Magic Of The Garden	Doreen Petherick Cox	185
Songs Men Sing	Deirdre White	186
The Amazon Aunt	Liz Davies	187
Waiting	Millicent Blanche Colwell	188
The Miracle Of Snowdrops	Doreen E Hampshire	189
Hillmorton	Diana Daley	190
Sweet Song Of Spring	Dorothy M Mitchell	191
Seascape	Hasan Erdogan	192
Promise Of Spring	Elizabeth Doroszkiewicz	193
Getting Away With Murder?	Tommy McBride	194
Untitled	Ann McLeod	195
Sweet Daffodil Song	Carol Ann Darling	196
Passing Seasons	Pat Spear	197
Autumn Leaves	Graham Watkins	198
Nature's Paradise - New Zealand	Helen Moll	199
God's Tapestry Of Love	Elizabeth Mason	200
The Tree	Henrietta Valmore	201
Calendar	Nigel Evans	202
The Law Of The Sea	Leigh Vickridge	203

The Poems

Summer's All

Warm winds that calm the golden breasts of summer
Seedy hours of heat
Village shows that come before the winter snows
Oh, did I drop off - did he score?
Some by sea relaxing on the shore
Strawberries and cream and baked to the core
All things good filling out to stack the winter store
Hours of tears and hours of joy
All things blended and complex
A journey between rise and fall
So much wanted, so much given
Wrapped in the happenings of still heat
Of afternoons at rest in time and place
Barbecues - parties - concerts and much more
Sensations, scents, shadows and nature's law
Sometimes summer smiles at you
Sometimes summer rages at you
Whatever summer is summer
Glorious are the memories of summers past
Whatever comes must go and will not last.

Clive Cornwall

Once Summer's Gone

I look at August, rain cascading down
Think of holidays spent at beach, begin to frown
Recall one particular time, huddled in coats:
Sheltering near stack of unused pedalo boats.

That week, height of summer, to sand we duly went
Our money on suntan lotion was never spent
In fact, no hot dogs, ice creams, doughnuts were required
Each day returned to caravan, crowded round fire.

Was this holiday made us make a decision
We'd take summer break in October from then on
Since that time we have been away once summer's gone
We've had great weather, pleasant memories live on.

Susan Mullinger

Capricorn Moon

I was looking for mercy
At the end of a rainbow
I was looking for the truth
In a pot of gold.

I was looking for the lies
That you never told
I was looking for snow in January
Under this Capricorn moon.

I found the solstice in December
I found failure in what I could no longer remember
I found joy in the darkest chords
And comfort in the harshest words
I found enlightenment in the dark
I found freedom in choices, which remained stark
All under this Capricorn moon.

I found bravery in my fear
I found courage in my tears
I found that there is no shame
In being glad to be alive
I found strangers and loved ones
In old sepia photographs
I found the lifeblood of dead
Musicians in old phonographs.

I found more than I thought I had lost
In the stillness of movement and time
I found new contours in the movement of a rhyme
I found more lies in walking a straight line
And new melody in a familiar tune
And I found meaning under the Capricorn moon.

Ben Macnair

First Summer

You are grown up now
And beside me make a
Complicated cake for your friend's birthday
Laden with the varied colours
Of the season's fruit.
I praise you
But know that no confection
Whatever its delicacy
Will compare with that of your first summer.

You, a baby
Watching me from your Moses basket
In the pom-pom tree's shade
The cat stretched asleep
At your side
In the wicker basket's dappled sunlight;
As I gather the early raspberries for you
Squeezing their softness into pieces
For your small mouth
Your tiny lips stained with juice.

. . . And later
Having dragged your light body
Round the kitchen, grasping my foot
As I mixed flour and eggs,
You clapped your hands
When I at last set the warm cake
In front of you:
The piled cream
Dripping, melted down the sides
As together we plopped the glistening berries
Glossy red
In your childish circle on top.

Karen Wood

Weather Wise

It's windy out there
And pouring with rain
Absolutely bucketing down
Beating on the windowpane.

Dare not venture out
Only get soaking wet
Wait until it eases
On that I wouldn't bet.

The chill makes me shiver
Cuts to the bones
Must have a cold coming
Can feel the undertones.

Come on. Pull yourself together
Shoulders back. Head held high
It's only a clearing up shower
Stop worrying. Come on. Try.

Put your head outside the door
That's right! Get it blown off!
Well look through the window
Can't see. The closeness makes me cough.

You going to sit here all day
Afraid of a drop of rain?
Yes, go on, mock me
Why get soaked? Nothing to gain.

I'll have another look later on
Give it time to stop and dry up
Just give me a few minutes
Get my good time spirits up.

It's not a day to be outside
Only a brave heart or fool will take a chance
Let me wallow in my dry parlour
By the coal fire giving merry dance.

William Stannard

Ever Wondered?

What wonders we can
See from the Earth
'Til the day we die
From the day of our birth
Such things as small birds and
Pretty dainty flowers
And ugly things
Like those big tall towers
All colours we view
Some we prefer more than others
And give flowers of 'their' favourites
To our loved ones or lovers
But we never actually think
What it would be
If all of these things
We could not see
For so many are out there
Yearning for sight
Just staring as though they
Are always looking into the night.

Marvyn Attwell

City

City to city
I can't find the link
To join this concrete
To this earth.
Still onward do we trudge
Watch the burning city sleep
See the trees gently grieve.
Draw me in
Stretch me out.
I'll never understand
What reasons abound
For bringing me here.

Clare Todd

The Millennium Year

The millennium year in springtime
Five planets in early May align in outer space
Is this a sign of seldom alliances
Between continents in spite of distances
To set rolling the balls of change?

The millennium year in summer
Three eclipses during July of the sun and the moon
Is this a sign of phenomenal changes
In technology, lifestyles and challenges
For an illuminating change?

The millennium year in autumn
One full moon in October on Friday the thirteenth
Is this a sign of natural disasters
Such as floods, earthquakes, tsunamis and twisters
For there being no instant change?

The millennium year in winter
One eclipse in December on a white Boxing Day
Is this a sign of the need for human spades
For buckets of snow of purifying aids
To effect the required change?

Eunice Ogunkoya

Summer In The Garden

Flowers are beautiful shrubs, kind of sweet
The way they all grow in the garden, pretty gorgeous and neat
The summer sun shines on grass, it feels so soft under my tiny feet
We can all sunbathe without a care
And put daisy chains in my hair
Buttercups under chin
Hey, I'm getting wet, we'll all run in
The hose is on
Water's getting in my shoe
But I'm still enjoying lying in the sun
Think I'll have a cup of tea and a nice cream bun.

Rosalind Ann Webb

Days In Mijas

A ship-shaped, high plateau, raised
up from the plains, the wastelands
her shore, the Sierra her chains.
Tall trees and ravines adorn
her in the breeze, as eagle-eyed
vistas glimpse ribboned blue seas.

Steep steps to perched villas, vine -
cladded and white that vie with
each other, defying the height.
But share in a flowering of
fragrant delights that cling and
cascade in their patios bright.

The square comes alive with the
'Al fresco' rites, of buying
and bronzing and doing the sights.
With cameras clicking all
over the town, the jaunty grey
donkeys trot daintily round.

They pose for proud parents of
children they host, their sad eyes
half-closed, their small hooves in repose.
But touring and traipsing through -
out the hot day, call for drinks
in the park as the sun dips away.

At night the town sparkles in
crescents of light, her towers
like funnels, glow out and invite.
High up in the mountains of
pine scents and sage, a spotlit
white chapel beams down from the range.

Rosemary Keith

Purification

Like a picture for a postcard
With the scene embossed by the sediment of sentimentality
The trees lie stipulated upon the sky
Albescent against the yolk of the sun
Residing low in the horizon
Splicing branches that have deshabilled their garments
Whilst we tighten ours and wear more
Surrounding the mystified pastures
Pasteurised by the midst of winter
Sterilising the earth
In order that it be revitalised
When snowdrops
As winter thaws
And the bluebells wring out
The tears of sorrow
From being bereft of colour
Tinged by the envy of spring
As a blanket of blue
Invigorates the bare wood
That canopies the summer
Creating a shade
That prevents the sun
From providing the light
That projects the spectrum
And so the blue blossoms
In a flourishing frenzy
Before being enclosed
In darkness
Until the wood relinquishes
Its colours to fall.

Anthony John Ward

Angel In A Cloud

Once upon a summer's day
I gazed toward the sky
And how my heart was filled with love
I know not how or why.

For in a cloud I saw her face
Angelic and divine
A special angel in a cloud
I felt somehow, was mine.

All through the day the cloud stayed near
Never lost from view
At times I heard a gentle sigh
That seemed to say, 'I'm here.'

I am your guardian angel
I'm never far away
In all your times of sadness
Close by your side I stay.

Jacqueline Claire Davies

Summer Symbols

There is no summer
But I can still smell the yellow roses
In my back garden
They play in my mind
In a calming breeze that never blows away
I can still see the zinnias
In the front lawn
Painting my life with colour
Summer's left without a word
But its creations remain
In the corridors of my mind
I can never be blind
To the symbols of summer
That have a lasting home in my thoughts

Muhammad Khurram Salim

A Wayward Child Of Mother Earth

A wayward child of Mother Earth
Cries as they cruelly debauch his mother's features,
Cries as they decimate his mother's creatures,
Cries as they rape her green fields
Lay waste to the contours of her lands,
And as they take healing from his mother's hands
Nature's child so bitterly cries.

A wayward child of Mother Earth
Seeks solace in the wilderness but finds nothing there,
Weeping now for his barren mother, the child is left alone -
Orphaned by 'progression'
The child is cast aside,
Child of a now dying line,
Empty.

A wayward child of Mother Earth
Slumbers deeply within his mother's womb,
But the Mother shall not travail in the pain of birth
Until those called 'civilised'
Have built their tomb.

And the children of Man's grave shall rise again . . .
I hear them whisper . . . don't you?
Nature's heart shall survive again . . .
I feel it pulsing . . . can't you?

Cerridwen

When Cerridwen opened the chasm of her mouth
She made me quake.
I remember feeling small as she rode upon the blue-black clouds,
Turquoise of the thunder-rods shimmering in her hands,
As she rolled towards conflict -
Towards him.

And behind me the searing heat of Taranis commands.
Bathing my back and the nape of my neck in ultraviolet fury,
His incandescent eye is focused, fixed,
Unwavering as he awaits her.
The Cailleach approaches in all her bruised cloud glory,
Song of the Morrigan serenading her,

He, in defence, burns ever brighter,
Attempting to evaporate her cool water
Into shards of rainbow-tinged mist.
He is proud. Erect. Strong for the moment.
He flares momentarily, then is gone
Devoured by her, shrouded by her.
Now joined in powerful union, the two opposing forces of
                                        Gaia's making

Consummate an almost reluctant love,
And then with light shot forth from her
They reach conclusion in ear-splitting tumult,
Then all falls silent.

Cerridwen retreats fulfilled and pregnant,
Carrying the Sun-Child who she nurtures until spring.
Taranis' light is weaker, the spent force heralds his decline,
But he shall be born again of her.
And I watch her disappear over the mountains,
Preparing for the completion of the ever-turning circle -
Love -
Birth -
Death.

Mark Marsh

Seashore

St Ives and Poole and Whitby and Wells
And sand and shore and soft seashells
And seagulls winging round and sounds
Of children watching merry-go-rounds.
And ice cream sellers filling cones
And swimming freaks in swimming zones
And mothers helping babies splash
And Father stripped out cuts a dash
And as we all loll on the shore
And hear the sound of the deep sea's roar
And know the joy of the things we saw
We appreciate the wealth of the wide seashore.

Joan Elizabeth Blissett

The Crying Seasons

Sudden dash of rain, devastated fields
The wind blows through the trees
But something is hurting their leaves
Strange and so sad feeling to hear and see

Could it be the chemicals in the air?
Though government has said and swears
To do something about the air's purity
Trees only like the serenity

Our beautiful trees are dying
And only a few people are despairing
Trees are being cut down
Some are being used in town

Tidal waves, wild angry wind
Roaring noises of a disturbed nature
No rain in African countries
Floods in cities for us, it is the future?

When will someone try to do right
Before we have trouble breathing day and night
Maybe everyone will start trying
Before the trees are gone and nature leaves us crying.

Victorine Lejeune-Stubbs

Earth's Love

Of golden sands
And cornfields
A copper-coloured sun.
Of oceans green
And skies of blue.
I talk
And walk
With you.

S A Brown

A Summer Day

In simmering sun I lie in quiet repose
The sounds of distant life doth borrow thought
As flickering light invites itself through leaves of oak.
I warm as birds call nigh as they from bough
To bough do dance a merry tune.
From garden pond they drink then sing anew
While busy bee no time to play but toil
And drink his nectar sweet
As angry crow dives down to scatter bird his victory won
He drinks with watchful eye till thirst is done
Relinquish not his post he sits and preens
Till daring sparrows take his throne
Adrift in tranquil peace I fly like fairy clocks
Upon the breeze and slumber not to miss
The fragrant smells of lingering blooms.
Take heed this day I share with birds and bees
Take not from me this rich bouquet of life
Till eventide dost don her cloak and all's at rest
I rise anon.

Joan Hosker

Yarmouth Beach

The fine top sand is blowing our way
As Taylor is covering his fingers as he plays
He crawls to where six sandcastles lay
It's a warm, sunny and breezy day.

Digging deep, it leaves a hole for Taylor to stand upright
He feels the sand around him so light
The kite flies in the wind with delight
And families are enjoying themselves, a happy sight.

Then after lunch, we must go for a paddle
But as the gentle waves roll in, will Taylor want a cuddle?
Later, leaving, we will push the pram with him asleep in the middle
Seeing out to sea, the working wind turbines to end this riddle.

Adrian Bullard

Elysian Fields

The night surrendered to a sphere of fire
The molten mass of morn's desire
And from it a sheet of opalescent-blue
Led crystal path to day's anew.

From the world the emerald-green
The vision of an Eireannach's dream
Burst forth to cover hill and vale
Gilt magic from a faerie tale.

And drifting 'cross the spellbound air
On secret wings so soft and fair
Bewitched an untamed melody
So rare the tune brought utmost glee.

A flock of forty thousand fliers
Rose full plume to lute and lyre
Whilst pixies waltzed and wood nymphs twirled
And epic tales from lips unfurled.

Creation in kind for all to thrive
As history from the future derive
A new era of life so fresh and bright
In moments, in mysteries, in wondrous delight.

Kristen Wood & Adam Poole

Games People Play

A cricket ball *thunks,* the girls peruse 'hunks'
And people set off with their towels and trunks
The sweat oozes out; little kids shout
While water officials begin to fear drought
Sun lovers don shades, sun haters find glades
As the gardener blasphemes his blooming blades
The umpire's decision provokes some derision
As the cricket lover is starved of his vision
Tennis players scan score - the golfer shouts, 'Fore!'
The British summertime is with us once more.

Warren Fraser

Secret Summer

Summer, the gentle hum of insects
Is carried on the gentle breeze
Leaves whisper
Soft, simple words of beauty.

The brook, low from long hot days
Bubbles and babbles, a trickle, clear, under the low bridge
Under the lychgate, on past church and farm
Following ancient tracks as in years long past.

How many have stood and looked
Have listened to the peace, and, with joy
Have marvelled at the wonders around them
Free to all?

A simple village, unchanged through time
So rich with beauty, so many have seen -
Born, lived, died, their lives forgotten
Except as part of the fabric, green.

Summer, endless in this secret place
Of time and mind
Never to be forgotten
Nor taken - stored in the memory
Of happy days.

Sue Wilson

Small Pleasures

'We went to the seaside Nanny, I saw lots of sea and sand
And I had a paddle in the water, my big sister held my hand.
We all went in the car, Mummy, Daddy, the baby, my big sister and me.
We left just after breakfast and got home in time for tea.
The sun was out, it didn't rain, I would love to go back there again.
Daddy says we can go back soon, after all, it's only June.'

Oh, the innocence of my granddaughter, who is only three
Proving small pleasures are there for everyone to see.

Maureen Arnold

Summer Sensations

S ummer skies and sunny days
U mbrellas protecting from sun's rays
M aking castles in the sand
M arching with the firm's brass band
E veryone, maybe, remembers these
R estless now though, more hard to please

S eeking destinations far away
E very kind of holiday
N ew horizons, foreign shore
S afaris, cruises, so much more
A ll in search of summer sun
T here are programmes to suit most everyone
I n search of romance, exciting, fast
O ver soon, they seldom last
N ow, travelled full circle, I prefer
S ummer's gentler sensations and holidays here.

Brenda Hughes

Summer Visitor

A huge tiny creature rests on my garden wall
Its fragile wings motionless
Its plump body sodden with summer heat
Rich, earthy-brown, bright buttercup-yellow
Alive in the sunlight.
Now rising lazily to creep into a curled-up bud
Gently pushing open the petals
Probing languidly
Amidst a velvet smoothness of peachy colour
Filling already bulging sacks of pollen
Rising now with fiercely flapping wings
Buzzing ferociously past my ear
Saying goodbye
Leaving a warm, restful memory of summer.

Muriel Nicola Waldt

View From The Low Path

Sunset and the soft glow of alyssum cushions
Lead the way
Mrs Pollock dressed in red and green
Holds up her tartan leaves in smart array.

Lupins there stand sentry-tall and strong
While star-faced little forget-me-nots
Shyly sprawl along.
Alliums hold maces
Fiercely guarding twig and leaf,

As towering sea holly shelters pansies underneath.
Some have gone to slumber
Petals closing like tired eyes.
While others fill the evening air

With perfume's soft surprise.
Their presence felt like magnetism
Pulsing from each flower
Each sense cocooned by the garden's breath
In this gentle twilight hour.

Miki Byrne

Summer Fun

The sun is shining gloriously
How lovely it is to sit in the park and just 'be'
Watching children riding their bikes in the sun
The little ones anxiously keeping an eye on Mum.

A picnic lunch causes much delight
Those children will sleep well tonight
A happy dog running around in the grass
I hope his excitement always lasts.

Teenagers playing football, yelling, 'It's a goal!'
Simply having fun, lifting the soul
Running past are keen joggers practising
Just watching the world go by, makes my heart sing.

Julie Marie Laura Shearing

Sunny

The early morning sun roused me from my bed,
The radio announcer said, 'There's a hot sunny day ahead.'
Our sunny summer days had really been such a few,
But Friday August 3rd 2007, proved to be absolutely true!

To meet a coach and my neighbour, I speedily did go,
Joining a queue of excited families, chatting in a long row,
Driving to the West Midlands Safari in Kidderminster, other coaches
we see
Arriving full of expectations, a day of joyful expectancy.

Slowly following the coach turning in front, the next hour was amazing.
Eagerly looking for animals, now asleep, the midday sun was blazing,
In their habitats of specially protected wide open spaces, they lay
Enjoying a siesta in the hot sunshine of this sunny summer day.

They advertised a big attraction, the New African Lion Family,
all pure white,
I heard all the 'oohs' and 'aahs' bringing the passengers great delight,
The surroundings were identical to a South African Safari I once knew,
Memories of a lookout tower I once climbed, wild animals to view.

Then for a wonderful sea lion display, we were just in time,
An arena packed with laughing children and parents, saw them
in their prime,
Two jumped their hoops and flapped their flippers and with their
keeper played
One called 'Wendy' barked correctly to questions, kids then
all hoorayed!

We moved on, discovering ten heavy hippos laying around a
large lake,
Gradually, these large dark creatures slowly moved, could barely
keep awake,
Suddenly went *splosh* into the water, after a meal of potatoes raw,
Standing on a bridge, everyone looked down, saw the keeper
throw them straw.

Finding dark, mysterious caves, as further on we walked,
Large tanks of swimming, colourful tropical fish, so interesting,
we talked,
Attractive shops, and thrilling roundabouts with 'screams and shouts'
we found,
Seeing ice creams, both bought one, doubles, costing only a pound!

Discovering wooden picnic benches, we relaxed, sat in the warm sun
Enjoying a drink and a sandwich,
Proved a day of 'sunny' summer sensations, for everyone.

Stella Bush-Payne

A Summer's Tale, Stratford-Upon-Avon

It was hot and stifling
in our thatched farm cottage,

perched side by side
on a narrow oak bench,

my family bustling in and out,
I gladly agreed when Will suggested a walk.

He brought me a pair of his father's cream leather gloves
for my 'porcelain-white hands'.

He was very talented,
wanted to give up teaching, write plays.

As we lay hidden in the apple orchard amongst long grass
how could I resist him?

Young and ardent
when he whispered his verse,

'Anne, shall I compare thee to this summer's day?
Thou art more lovely and more temperate.'

We're wedding next week by special licence.

Carole Luke

Butterfly Ridge

Just outside the town of Bundaberg
Off the east Australian shore
Is a high point called The Hummock
A rare beauty spot to adore.

To the right of the Hummock scenery
Is a home-built wooden bridge
Leading to a wooded glade
And named, The Butterfly Ridge.

Having crossed the narrow walkway
Just wide enough for one
A journey into wonderland
For a visitor has begun.

Through a shaded pine-filled forest
Tropical trees with palm-type leaves
Honeysuckle-shrouded bushes
Add their scent to the cooling breeze.

Treading deeper through the wooded glade
An air of silence to be found
Behold, a wondrous sight appeared
Butterflies, a hand's-breath wide
Descending all around.

Their colours were breathtaking
As they floated through the air
Mixed colours of the rainbow
Their winged patterns did compare.

Purple Emperor, a Chalkhill Blue
Clouded Yellow, to name a few
Like gentle fairies they came to rest
Upon one's garment worn
Friendly, soft and delicate
Like a being newly born.

While observing this creation
Thoughts might develop in the mind
That if these butterflies could speak
What message would we find?

'Come forth to view our kingdom
If 'peace' be the world you seek.
Butterfly Ridge will welcome all those
Who cross its Hummock creek.'

Ernest Hannam

That Sunny Day

It was like this, one sunny day,
That we all waited for fate to play
One of her tricks that, sometimes,
We know will change our lives
And the way we must go.
There you were, so young that day,
Laughing, with one of your tricks to play,
That I fell backwards, into the sand,
But, you rescued me with a strong, quick hand.
Then I was lost, as our eyes that met
Gave me a thrill I could never forget.

The sand is still here, and the sea so strong,
But you, my love, are now long-gone
On that tide of war, that swept you away,
Gallant and laughing, still at play.
But, I remember and will not forget
The love in my heart is forever set,
Ready, and waiting, just for that day,
When we shall meet, as I know we will,
For that last and never-ending thrill,
The destiny that is meant to be,
The lasting heaven, for you and me.

Mary Hughes

Holidays

They say
The 'rain in Spain lies mainly on the plain'
I've been there and will not go back again
Nor Germany, nor France or Italy
I find that Blackpool does for me
Where I've spent many a pleasant hour
Atop the Blackpool Tower
The thrills of the funfair
I've had some great times there
Don't yearn for French champagne or German hock
Me, I like the taste of Blackpool rock
Why go round the world to take a holiday?
Now Blackpool, I can get there in a day
So you feel free, far lands to roam
Me - I'll holiday at home!

Gordon Andrews

Visions

Bewitched by the mist
As slowly it crowns
Engulfing the sides of the great South Downs
No longer can be seen
Those hills of old
As the mist sweeps lower
It will us too enfold
Blessed with vivid powers of mystique
Gone again, are the walkers' feet
The bracken is green and soft below
Full of colour, are the orchids I know
The trees remain idle
And momentarily, all is still
Suddenly, the sun starts shining back through
Revealing the sky in its July summer-blue.

Linda Wilson

Speculation

It was high summer and the sun
Was warm upon my face
As I walked on the shore.
I was going to meet a boy
I had met the night before.

He was tall and handsome
In a craggy sort of way,
I hoped he would be there
Near the rocks.
Kicking the sand
I looked up at the clouds
Caressing the adjacent cliffs,
The imagery was mirrored in a rock pool.
A solitary heron ruffled the surface
Breaking the illusion.

But that was no illusion
I had seen in the distance
There he was walking towards me
With a feeling of elation
I ran towards him
And knew this was going to be my day.

Rosaleen Clarke

June 21st

Today is the summer solstice
in the northern hemisphere
but Morningside is not full
of bearded Druids in white nightgowns,
brandishing mistletoe.

Today is the longest day of the year when
the Earth's axis tilts at over 23 degrees
and the noonday sun reaches its zenith.
What does this mean in practice? Rain
pissing down again. Like yesterday. Like the day before.

Norman Bissett

Away With The Fairies

The raindrops on the water,
The sunlight through the clouds,
Show colours of the rainbow
Like flowers in silken shrouds.

We reach out through the raindrops
To touch this fine array,
But the flowers become fairies
And then they fly away.

The breeze brushes our faces
From their tiny silver wings,
Such peace and tranquillity
Their mystic presence brings.

We cannot always see them
But we know when they are there,
We can sense it in the silence
And the magic in the air.

If you are really lucky
One still midsummer's eve,
They may come to visit you
. . . If you just believe.

Kath Cooley

Tree Leaves

In summer they are
full of colour

In autumn they are
brown and yellow

In winter they are
none to be seen

In spring they are
reborn and sweet.

Bav

School Holidays

Every year at summertime
The kids get out of school
For 'alleged' weeks of sunshine
And swimming somewhere in a pool.

Lists are made in the first few days
And stuck inside the cupboard door
So hopefully we will never hear the words,
'Hey Mum and Dad, we're bored.'

Places of possible interest
Are noted throughout the year
Safari Park or Deep Sea World
Should maybe bring some cheer!

We do like all being together
And all get on well as a rule
Though soon going away with Mum and Dad
Will be seen as quite 'uncool'.

When the kids get sick of each other
They like to have friends round
With water fights on the back lawn
With excited shrieks and sounds.

The summer weeks have just flown by . . .
And you know the holidays are almost through
When we spend an entire morning
Just choosing new school shoes!

Chris Leith

Last Summer - Haiku

The long sunny days
Quickly fade to memories
Of days now long past.

Johana West

Endless Summers

How I dream about us going back in time
To those endless summers,
When time seemed to stand still
As if waiting for us to catch up;
And when we watched sunsets
They were like fired mirrors
Full of our passion and desire.

Then, it was forever, or so it seemed
There were no signs of pain or fear.
Both of us sweated for want of each other
Our fingers slipping often into the unknown,
Exploring forbidden crevices . . . of life
Hoping these were the ultimate moments,
Until we lay side by side breathless
Trying to come to terms with what seemed
Lawless, immoral or even a crime;
Our love was berserk.

I remember you then, in your light blue shorts
Which you wore so teasingly to provoke
Showing off your sun-tanned curves.
I can still see you as if it were yesterday,
Only yesterday was thirty years ago.
. Now, I wonder about your satin-black hair,
If it still flows down to your naked waist
And if you still swing your head from side to side
Like in a flowing samba rhythm.
Often, you used to catch me
From the corner of your eye drooling
And you would smile almost sadistically,
And pull your hair to one side
With your delicately thin fingers
Letting it flow onto my bare chest.

I inhaled your perfume
As if it were the essence of life
Or an elixir of immortality,
Never daring to wash it off
Until I made certain you returned, that night
That night in secret silence,
While shushing my enthusiasm
Afraid our love would fade like the silver moonlight
In which we basked so often,
Until it turned pale and invisible.

No one knew of our secret love then,
Of our illicit desire to rest in each other's arms
Spending those youthful nights
Until they turned grey with age.
When we touched, it was like an electric shock,
Our hearts beat so fast I often thought
The thumping would give us away.
Your sighs and my sighs seemed so loud,
Too loud to stifle into the darkness.

Until the world around caved in unexpectedly on us
And we broke apart into divided worlds.
How I would like us to go back in time together
If it was not for the fear we would linger on,
Perhaps, even choose a different path
Never to return, never to be what we are today.

Ray Fenech

July

J uly and I'm on holiday
U llswater sparkles in the sun
L ooming clouds, approaching storm
Y ou kiss me and our love is born.

Joyce Walker

Summer Isn't Over Yet

S oothing waters cooled my skin
U nder blazing sunrays
M y skin turned golden and radiant
M y hair highlighted and wispy
E very hour of the day filled with
R elaxation and carefree feelings

I sn't it wonderful how we all feel young in the sun?
S cents filled my nose and reminded me of childhood days
N ot needing to worry of going back to work
T rawling the pier stalls with pockets full of pennies

O nly worrying how high my sandcastle would be
   and Grandad getting me that toy from the
V ending machine that nobody could win
E verybody smiling, it
R eally was a wonderful time

Y es, those days are gone, but they are replaced with kissing
   in the dunes
E ating out in the balmy evenings at beach barbecues with friends
T asting the salt on each other's lips when we kiss
   and returning to the quaint B&B room to make love.

Sarah Louise Dermody

Summer Secrets

The eagle soars above the craggy dawn
Of a land filled by strangers
The sea envelops the mountains of Mourne
And the spray that rains saturation
Catches the unsuspecting of love
Caressing the waves of candescent beauty
The dusk approaches with fresh-flung danger
As midsummer murders of jilted lovers
Seek revenge on the elements
Meanwhile, the sun burns a hole in the sky
Denoting the gods are still watching.

Finnan Boyle

Forward Press - Nature's Paradise

Summer

Sweet scents of honeysuckle and roses
Wafting gently through the air;
Children playing happily
Without a care;
Holidays in far-off places,
Breathtaking sights and friendly faces;
Migratory birds from distant shores
Have returned to greet us all once more;
Lovers walking hand in hand
On balmy nights under moonlit skies;
Family picnics in the park
And staying out till after dark;
Lazy afternoons sipping lemonade,
Finding a perfect spot in the shade;
The buzzing of bees and wasps
And an explosion of new life;
Cooling down with ice cream
On sultry, dreamy, summer days.

Annabelle Tipper

Whispering

As the flower gently bends towards me
Whispering of the new season to come
Rolling mists that bring dew in the morning
Feeling that chill in the air

They were only dreams yesterday
Autumn's tapestry of colours
Bathing in the autumnal glow of today
Ah, wonderful colours of life

Whispering flower of summer's hue
Gone so soon, to sleep till spring
To bloom your welcome for summer days
Sleep now, grow strong for your welcome return

Wonderful colours, signs of a season new.

Carole A Cleverdon

A Summer Storm

Low clouds were slung across a slate-grey sky,
Rolling and pitching like a stormy sea.
Their tenuous forms, with furious friction jostled,
Had charged the air with electricity.

Then fearful cracks of fire split the heavens,
Lighting the ether with a silver glow
And giant hammers, thrown from Vulcan's forge,
Resounded on the stricken world below.

Now nebulus vapours floated down to Earth
Concealing mountain tops in swirling mist,
And stately oaks were swallowed in the gloom
As if they were unable to resist.

Powers of raindrops pulverised the fields,
Flailing the corn with Herculean might
And blooms were beaten down with brutal force,
Their fragrant beauty lost without a fight.

Rabbits scampered back into their burrows
And squirrels chittered as they sought their dreys.
Annoyed by this inopportune confusion
They longed for the return of sunny days.

At last the rainbow, there for all to see,
Renewed the binding promise He had made.
Its iridescent arc joined Earth to Heaven
But soon its transient loveliness would fade.

Celia G Thomas

Summer Skies

I love to see those billowing clouds
Sunlit from above
Rising higher, ever higher
As if on wings, those of a dove.

Oh, if I could climb those dazzling heights
Those mountains in the sky
Would I ever reach the range
Where all sense of time would die?

Would I scale a snow-white cloud
Then descend into a vale
To climb again and find another
That gives such brilliant visual pleasure?

Would my path from Earth's horizon
Lead on such an awesome trail
That I would pause in praise and wonder?
Infinity only can prevail.

I have flown above the billows
And seen the rising of the sun
But on a sunny summer's day
It's on Earth that I belong.

Ah, those lovely billowing clouds
Against the heavenly-blue
I see again, as I look down
Reflected, in my little garden pool.

Agnes Hickling

Castaway

Today, as I strolled along the beach with the smell of the sea
                                                    tantalising my nose,
A soft breeze ruffling sun-bleached hair, and the feel of sand
                                                    between my toes,
I started to think that perhaps it was time to find some means
                                                    of escape from this place
Where I'd been marooned for several weeks, having disappeared
                                                    without a trace.
So tomorrow I'll start to construct a vessel - an ocean-going craft,
Like a small canoe or coracle, or perhaps even a raft.
Yes, tomorrow morning I'll rise with the sun and make an early start,
And, with any luck, when my craft is complete, I'll be ready to depart.
But, with the dream now a reality, as I sit by a driftwood fire
Which makes reassuring crackling sounds as the flames leap
                                                    higher and higher,
I'm beginning to wonder if my plan to leave this island -
                                which now feels like home -
Was such a great idea after all, as I've become used to being alone.
The thing is, I've grown sort of fond of this place
And quite like the feel of the sun on my face
As it filters through the leaves of the palms
And casts flickering shadows on my bare legs and arms.
So, perhaps I'll postpone my boat-building until another day
And continue to live on my paradise isle - there's every good reason
                                                    to stay;
For the diet of fish and coconut milk seems to suit me - I feel so alive!
After all, I've been here for many weeks now, so I know I can survive.
So, as another day draws to a close, mesmerized by the smoke
Swirling from the fire, with the darkness wrapped around me
                                like a soft, velvet cloak
Beneath a canopy of stars, I'm gently lulled to sleep
By the sound of water lapping, just inches from my feet.

Heather Pickering

Vagary Vacation

Here at last the long anticipated summer
I can now dispose of my threadbare jumper
While harvest crops can still be termed a bummer -
Crash course at the gym for in the mirror I look plumper.

I scan finances to formulate my plan
What place will receive the custom of this weary man?
Skegness, Cleethorpes, Mablethorpe, could be also ran
I plump for Malta, let the others go down the pan.

Off I set with suitcase labelled and bulging
With camera loaded I anticipate indulging
The chemist's shop is where I've been trudging
Sun Factor 5 is the barrier in which I am trusting.

Seven days in the sun, that's done the trick
If I'd been to Blackpool they would 'Kiss Me Quick'
Rock is at a premium, I didn't see a stick
I avoid the boat rides, they might make me sick.

Time to go home now the holiday is over
I have to wrench myself free from the arms of my lover
Holiday romances are a bit of a bother
Still, it was nice while it lasted, now it's back to my mother!

Postcards have been posted with views of the island
Question I pose is will they land before I land?
There was plenty of water but not that much sand
If there's anything I've forgotten, it's out of my hand.

Arriving back in Manchester I can't believe there's still rain
My baggage I pick off the carousel causing some strain
The transport I ordered is not there, it's a bit of a pain
Holidays in future, I will go on the train.

John Waby

Summer Chats

Who is summer?
What is summer?
Take away all nature's glories
The sun, the stars
The precious blue skies
And the sea of bathing blue
You'll bound to hear
'Oh how dull
Summer is so rubbish this year'
But when the children
Are happy in their play
Boisterous noises
And fun galore
Many faces would light up
And a flow of words
Would roam the air,
'Oh we had a very happy summer
This year.'

Carolie Cole Pemberton

Barcarolle

Glistening in the sunshine
The lapping water is placid and deep
Against the buildings, ancient
Tall, broad and wide
The verandas, the shutters
Are closed from the noonday heat
The single oar, slim, black and long
Moves the graceful barque majestically along
Elegant and light, the Venetian gondola
Is led by the spirited marinaio
At the stern of this medieval vessel
Histoire Italienne comes together
In this vivacious scene
This watery setting of palaces
Barges, bridges and campaniles.

Margaret Bennett

In British Summertime

There are a few minutes
On the odd evening
In British summertime
When the light outside seems unreal
When the sun has gone down below the houses
But the sky
Seems desperate to hold on to the day
Radiating all its light
Until it's nothing left
And the clouds seize their moment
Creating nothing but a wet blanket
To tuck us in for the night
As our unfortunate part of the Earth
Turns its back on the sun for a few hours more
And it rains again
Like it always does
And another day is gone.

Matt Doran

Sonnet: I Remem'er

The sun of late summer and songs I hear
This fine morning and freedom that I long
I told the truth and you forgot the tear
I shed and now I think of what was wrong
When in the light of day the songbird sings
I look upon myself and then wonder.
Here by and by, I live for what life brings
Come, my sweet life, away distant thunder
I remem'er the sunset, twilight
At the end of day and what a moonlight it
Was. Now, I realise the artful mat
The stars are out and so the sky is lit
If love is by, then love is all in me
If love is not, I still can serve and see.

Jasmine Kang

Tree Time

Tick . . .
Another year ends, here and there, another begins
Blossoms emerge from their constricting bud
Incense-like fragrances fill the air
Bushes, trees and shrubs are a kaleidoscope of colour.

Tock . . .
A bursting sun stands high upon its arc
Beaming forth rays of tropical heat
Children take the risk, running over hot sand into the sea
Laughing, playing, splashing, cool and fresh.

Tick . . .
A distant sun behind the horizon
A chill hangs in the vast clear air
Coloured leaves on the trees, fall
And become a weary colourful carpet of rotting leaves.

Tock . . .
Blue skies shrouded from view, gathering dark clouds
Rain, wind, thunder, lightning, snow and ice
Snowy days really are nice
How simple can it all be
To see a day as it should be.
This is my watch, this is my year
As for the numbers . . . I don't really care.

Richard Lyes

Daddy Bunchie

Blowing Daddy bunchies
Clear blue swallow skies
Bendy corncockle breezes
Jelly bean sandal pies
Twirly bird spinning sycamores
Sticky bud thistles fly
Rosa Rugosa glory
Lambing season high.

Dranoel Yengid

Emma's Cottage

I used to dread the summer sun
Always hot and sticky
Our reflections if possible, visible on the hot
Tarmac under the wheels of another car
Piling up to 'somewhere nice'
Fragmented images of excitement,
Boredom and longing to get away
To be free of the long roads
And smog-filled city.
Now I love that very experience
The adventure of somewhere to go to
Away from life's mundane drag
Watching grey turn to green and longing
For that cottage with its history
Warmth and charm.
Escaping to the lush grass of
Its garden and the table under
The evening sun, quietly awaiting
The arrival of my wine and I.
Another summer rolling away
With no care for today or tomorrow
Or more importantly, yesterday.

Karen Zena Roberts

Crowhurst

When we came down to Crowhurst
On a glorious summer's day
The blackbirds were flying in unison
The grass was ready for hay
Oh ay they are singing for summer
Oh ay for the sky is blue
Oh ay for the sick are healed
And they're sailing a big canoe.

Peter Alfred Buss

Lunar Promise

That summer, the nights of heat, not flood
Unable to rest or sleep, no intimate touch
We took a drive beyond the urban walls
Beyond bubbling tarmac and circling cars
Beyond frayed nerves, exhaust haze
Beyond music and city threats.

We broke through, past parched fields
Watched swallows dart from cool nests
And jink to chase heat-mad moths
Climbing from the listless village pathways
Climbing by deco vases in shop gloom
Where dustmites stirred and beetles scuttled.

Up along steep, rising, rutted roads
We pulled away from the valley's heavy heart
And wilted hedgerow flowers and thirsty trees
Parking at the highest moorland point
With silence, sheep and rustling gorse
And watched the cool moon rise, promising autumn.

David Reddall

A Summer Shower

A summer shower of refreshing rain
Leaves everywhere fresh and new again
Strong aroma of woodland smells
Leaving lots of the animal tell-tale trails
Animals frolicking through flooded paths
Enjoying late evening summer baths
Puddles galore, the stream's now full
Enable everyone to cool
From the daytime heat of the blistering sun
Which begins to fade now the day is done.

Summer brings its memories and so much more
Soon autumn will be knocking upon the door.

Christine Hardemon

The Treasures Of Darkness

'Tis late summer, the sun blazing in the azure sky
Geese in formation flight overhead, a noisy departure
Dividing into a V, behind two leaders, soaring high
To the depths of the Earth, we follow our leader
The brochure said, 'find yourself in Fermanagh, in the
European Geopark'
And so, to the cool interior of a cavern to 'find ourselves'
Floodlit, for otherwise, like 'finding ourselves', it could be very cold and
very dark.

A veritable fairy wonderland, calcite walls, a subterranean river
Which reflected rock-strewn floors and shimmering terraces
Gleaming stalactites and stalagmites, some cauliflower-shaped
Some, meeting midway, to form a wedded pair
The addition of each glistening dewdrop, day by day
And through the centuries, year by year!

Away from the clamour and the rush
To the order and peace at the heart of creation
This summer held a fresh experience for us
And one we will repeat, if spared
Overcoming the fear of closed in spaces
He who dares wins, and he who wins dared!

Beryl Moorehead

Summer

Summer is a lovely time
I take the kids to the parks at bay
Many rides, space for exciting play
Picnics at bay, we all tuck in
Have great days
Then pile in car at bay
Tired, ready for our beds at bay.

D McDonald

Childhood

I looked in my grandmother's memory and found:
An ice cream scoop that wobbled on my lip
Nasturtiums where insects came to sip
A wave that broke in cups on a beach trip.

I looked in my father's memory and found:
Bare toddler's feet, splish-sploshing in a pool
Lessons of hare and owl in nature's school
A trout that leapt and changed into a jewel.

I looked in my mother's memory and found:
Red sandals that must not be scuffed or scratched
A meagre joy that must be earned not snatched
A golden field where winter shadows hatched.

I looked in the sun's memory and found:
A meadowland that rippled like a sea
A galleon in the top branch of a tree
Freedom to run outwith the bounds of me.

Sheena Blackhall

The Beach

As we walk across the uneven pebbles,
A gentle wind circulates a summer heat,
The air filled with squeals of laughter,
Before our eyes a rippling of the blue sea,
Buckets and spades deserted by moulded sandcastles,
Sodden towels sprawled out by upright deckchairs,
Children plastered in suncream, head to toe,
Knotted hankies cover balding heads,
Curling crusts of sandwiches await the hungry gulls,
Discarded drink cans fill the overflowing bins,
The sun starts to retire, the beach empties,
Stillness blows across the once-packed sand,
Memories kept on spools of film,
People at home, the beach now a distant memory,
Another summer passes by!

Carol Paxton

Summer Chameleon

Peculiar shadows erupt across the skies
The summer breeze dances through the trees,
Waving the branches and the leaves.
Temperatures plummet,
As hostile rain disturbs the peace.

Birds fear the scenes
Flying swiftly to hide,
And not be seen,
For this summer chameleon seems very keen.

Cats find the summer chameleon baffling
But they don't complain,
Because they don't know who to blame.
Is it the Devil or God?
Or the sin of Cain?

No one will ever understand the summer chameleon
Or the disharmony it brings,
Because it is such an unexpected thing.
Where next will it swing?

I recall blissful summers of the past
Stress-free, contented and relaxing; having
Beautiful sunrises, humid days and wonderful sunsets.
On the beach people sunbathe,
With children playing and dogs stick chasing.

Sunshine brightens the sky for ten minutes,
Then gloomy clouds darken it.
Summer chameleon plays its games,
And so goes the merry-go-round.

Ali Sebastian

Seasonal Touch

Seasons create the motivation, of the years
An assurance has been established, through our peers
Spring, summer, autumn, winter, influencing time
We humans, earnestly watch for the positive sign

The sign which indicates *spring,* is at last here
Enrich the soil till and toil, for plants to reappear
Seed is sown, with tender care, hopeful for results
Green shoots appear, the gardener's triumph, is exult

Then comes *summer,* which often takes its time
An illusion, perhaps one day the sun will shine
Followed by insistent rain, creating sad depression
Spirits wane, the sun happily shines, assuring its intention

Autumn shades commence, to fill the dells with colour
Shades of the most enduring blends, enhancing every borough
Fruits are visible, after speculation and daunting wonder
Apples, nuts, berries, all appear, many in a fine cluster

Winter, suddenly arrives, temperature says cold
Time for reminiscing, on what the seasons controlled
Looking back with hindsight, agreed it's not been bad
Time, instigates production, rejoice, smile, be glad.

Lorna Tippett

Vista Views

Ice and winds
Heart in the middle
Of a season's rain.
The lonely skies
The bloom head of morning.
In silence with nature
A drugged experience.
Vista in tranquillity
With lonely spaces within
The nursed sorrows.

Roger Thornton

Summer

I remember a day last summer
One special day last June
Everyone seemed so happy
Even birds sang in tune.

I took a walk along our street
And was pleased where I put my feet
All seemed so very friendly
As we sat and talked upon a seat.

So today is a very nice one
The sun is oh so hot
Time I took some clothes off
But there again, I'd better not!

But, oh too soon, summer is over
And then the clocks will be put back
Soon we'll have the winter
But please don't remind me of that.

David Sheasby

Fun In The Sun

How fortunate it is, my family
Reside in Florida, the Sunshine State,
Upon an island, circled by the sea,
A paradise, in which to ambulate,
Or swim, or boat, sunbathe, relax, unwind,
For younger folk there's tennis and there's golf,
Though, at my age, I've left those sports behind,
My object being just to spoil myself,
Forget my cares, enjoy my family,
Make every precious moment with them count.
I walk the dogs, play with them in the sea,
Have so much fun, it's too much to recount.
Come evenings and the awesome sunset red,
A cooling drink, a barbecue, then bed!

Christopher Head

Summer Expectations

Anticipation: of long, hot, lazy days
Spreadeagled on a sandy beach
Sunglasses, suncream, shady hat
A cooling drink within arm's reach.

Would there be sizzling romance
Under a full moon or golden sun?
Perhaps mixing with a carefree crowd
Dancing, laughing, having fun?

Ah, off at last to join the motorway -
Delays, cones, roadworks, crawling traffic
Everyone gets grumpy, bad-tempered, bored -
Then - final straw - *the dog is sick!*

Relentlessly the sun beats down -
The car becomes an oven and so smelly.
Exhausted we arrive, glad to be there
But - where, oh where, is beach and sea?

Oh yes, it is there, but so far off -
We should have brought our hiking shoes!
Well, never mind, it's just a blip
But - Father's now on a short fuse!

We wake next morning, skies are grey
And rain is simply teeming down
Brought our macs? Of course we didn't
So drift despondently around the town.

We must have chosen a bad week
As day by day it is the same
The rain pours down from leaden skies -
We wonder why we ever came?

The weather has affected staff
A most *unhelpful* bunch are they
Simple requests are turned down flat -
You feel as if you're in the way!

At last the week drags to an end
Sadly, unused bikinis are repacked -
We join the queue all homeward bound
And get back late, completely whacked!

We wake next day to hot, hot sun
And suntanned friends pop in to say
With the heatwave of all last week
How *lucky* we were to be away!

Joyce Hockley

August 2007

Oh endless skies of leadened grey
A biting wind to make it cold
One year ago we basked in sun
Ah halcyon days of golden brown!

The tide has turned - we reach for macs
(Plastic) as the raindrops fall
The British Summer is awash
With careful plans - quite ruined now.

Deserted are the miles of sands
Like Yarmouth/Weston-super-Mare
Donkeys wait in vain for crowds
Who flock inland to leisure pools.

Our tourism is battered too
(Bed and breakfasts - empty rooms)
Returning home has been a flood
From Devon, Cornwall and elsewhere.

Let's dip a toe in future hols
(Those Latin seas - so azure blue)
Forget these past few soggy months
Pore over brochures out today.

Steve Glason

Darkness Descends on Upton-Upon-Severn

Darkness descends on Upton-upon-Severn
A breeze caresses her golden hair
Liquid velvet river placid as a pond
Boats' reflections painting
The impotent summer water
As the lads and their girls laugh so carefree
Drinking and smoking on the stony quay.

I gently squeeze her fretful hand
The passion-jewelled eyes just memories
And although this is a beautiful place
I now stare at empty beer cans
Cigarette butts strewn asunder
And a sad old man on a seat alone
Future mirror, I look back, he is gone.

Darkness descends on Upton-upon-Severn
Music and voices drift ghost-like from the bar
And King of Clubs illuminated
And the water, now sinister, seems to call me
But the pub is where I'll drown tonight
For when she's lying in our loveless room
I'll jinx the happy hordes . . . yet sit in gloom.

Guy Fletcher

Dancing Snowflakes

The sun is warmly bright at noon, in a sky of clearest blue.
But soon the winter day will end, and the forecast is for snow!
A crimson sunset beyond the trees, with their branches of lacy black.
The final shadows disappear along the woodland track.

Now the sky is midnight-blue, pin-pricked with a thousand stars.
Then clouds rush in from the northern hills, and they are lost to view.
In the three/four time of an old-fashioned waltz the snowflakes

first appear.
Feather-light, crystal-white, they dance through the icy air.

Meryl Champion

Storm Brewing

A blistering sun beats down remorseless
The land parched, every grain of heated sand
Sucks dry the moisture rendering the sky cloudless
Mirage shimmers of ascending thermals in seamless band
Rise to the cool ramparts seeking a celestial rest
Nature's invisible conduit of suction at its behest.

The waters of the ocean in silent turmoil froth and fume
Lather whipped by sub-sea currents, the surface wind detach
This vapour stream extracted the heavenly lung consume
Mushrooming in bellicose vein the nimbus layers attach
A veritable monster, flexing charged muscles, steadily grows
Unmitigated hunger in its tormented belly, the thunder growls.

The sun now in its southern journey bestows a slanted glance
Cool northern breeze, heavy and lethargic in wintry slumber
Is rudely awakened, an alluring invitation to a heated dance
Twirling in frenzy the twosome meets in an annihilating number
Contagious their fervour the heavenly breath in crescendo soar
Passion rising consummates their ardour in a thundering roar.

Barnabas Tiburtius

Summer Sensations

Full soared the clouds, dramatic, free
Lined beyond green hedge and tree
Drama suspended at a glance
An expanse of rippling sea to dance
Ever-roving and ships to thrill
Yachts; red sails billow outward with a will
At the water's edge a seaweed shelters in
Where lullabies upon the beach begin
Watch more again at a sensual tide
Waves of volume higher and higher which stretch so wide
Another cornet heaped with cream
Gazed by townfolk who laze and dream
Those steps and uphills near the shores
Captivate the livery and beaches at Saint Mawes.

Tom Cabin

The Sun

The sun was sinking fast
In the western sky
So soon the sun was up
That it was passing by
It started bright and cheerful
With it rising in the east
Bringing a golden glow
On which one's eyes could feast
Like a canopy it spread
To a point that's overhead
Then casting shadows everywhere
Slowly sank again to bed
So quick the day was gone
Just in the blink of an eye
So live each day to the full
Before life passes by.

Daphne Fryer

Forever Summer

Winter, black and white
displaces, disposes of me briefly,
instead I trespass into dreams
of vibrant summer hues
and stare with joy
at sunshine reflected
in the mirrors of my mind.

Fragmented are the
many shades of summer
for me to stitch a
patchwork quilt of light
transport it into winter
and curl inside
to feel the sun.

Isabel Cortan

Waiting For A Lecture

Blue skies
Fresh green leaves
Red roofs
Brown cottages
Springy grass
Open windows
Sitting by
Knitting blue wool
Palm trees
Come to mind
By sandy beaches
Skimpy clothing
Bright sunny day
Warm, but breezy
Back to the present
Martha, Anne, Ayo and I
Standing here
Under a tree
Waiting for a lecture.

Debra Ayis

Lost Spirit

It's very odd
And sometimes frightening
To see
A vivid flash of lightning

You feel
That when you hear the thunder
God's cross today
Who's made a blunder?

It could be one
Who didn't know
Who at Heaven's gate
Should have gone below!

Joan Hammond

Settle In Seattle

And still the summer sun does shine
Even though it's wintertime
Ever since you said you were mine
And though the air is getting colder
With each day I get bolder
I cannot wait till I get older
Till the summertime.

When you said we'd settle in Seattle
Where the air is nice and clear
But I wanna be travelling onward
I want to go home, no more to roam.

If you say you don't want to come with me
All I can do is leave without you
And say that we are through
But I don't want to go home without you
Don't want to roam alone, so pick up a phone
And marry me this wintertime.

And don't say we'll settle in Seattle
Where the air is nice and clear
I wanna be travelling onward
I want to go home
No more to roam
I want to go home.

Philip John Loudon

Stirred Memories

Uninterrupted clear skies
Sunset on the town's green
At the end
Of a perfect high August day
Skies changing colour
From blue to shades of reds
Hush calm of evening tide
First stars twinkle up high
In the Milky Way
Evening cooler, refusing air
A bonus treat
Relief from sweltering day's heat.

Sit back, relax in a fold-up chair
Taking in the scene
On the town's green
Listening to silky sounds
Of orchestral music
The prom smooth one being
Musical notes of Green Sleeves blend
With a typical English scene
Making one aware of whom
We are
Stirring faraway memories
Of lovely summer days gone by.

Bryan Clarke

The Farm

There is a stoop and a step,
And a studded door,
And a stone-flagged path
To a summerhouse floor,
Where shafts of sunlight
Slant to a hidden store
Of old, old things going back
Five centuries or more.
And in the walled garden
There stands an apple tree,
Its fruit sweet to the very core.
A horse waits tranquil by the gate
And flints from far-off shores
Form walls of peace under slate
And roofs that slope to lead gutters,
And the wood pigeon upward flutters;
Beak full of late nesting stuff.
And there we are, my twin soul and I,
Knowing a lifetime here
Will never be enough;
Picking sloes softly till twilight
And the warm embrace of
A wood fire by candlelight.

Joan Woolley

Summer Storm

A flash
Suddenly crashed
A cloud of easeful ink
When the belly
Of a burning heart
Trembled
Upon the awakening
Of a dream

All the scallops
Clustered
When the pearls
Painfully squirmed
Beneath the chaos
And turbulence

I love you, Summer
While the absence
Of my light
Devastated your flowers
And a riot
Befell your meadows
Amidst the cliffs
And your dolce voice.

David Lin

Dream Away A Summer's Day

The yacht bounced gently on the waves
The sails flapped in the breeze
The peace and quiet of a summer's day
My eyes closed on the open seas
Then clouds began to appear above
Intriguing shapes formed in the sky
I heard the thud of galloping hooves
As horses came thundering by
Their long flowing manes and tails held high
Such beauty I had never seen
Strong and powerful with nostrils of fire
Shining coats, rippling and lean
They ran at speed with joy in their hearts
Then suddenly they floated away
I awoke to see a lovely blue sky
On a beautiful summer's day.

Catherine Mary Armstrong

Picturesque

A rustic village nestles by a spring,
Dappled by the golden shafts of morn
The oak, rheumatic with knotted joints,
Shades springing grass and nodding flowers.

Early songbirds serenade the clearing sky,
The breath of blossoms linger as a lover's kiss
Upon the lips of the morning.

Luring the honeybee
A haunting fragrance through a window blows,
Softly scented apple and cherry blossom.

The first sweet rose blooms
And spends its perfume on the air,
Mayflower curtains drift to touch the floor.

Beverly Maiden

Gemini Bay

Shades of orange abound in Gemini Bay
Flickering tongues of fire
Dance and play,
The glow of dawn
The start of a brand new day.

Marmalade horses stoop to kiss the shore
As they run amok
Upon a lemon floor,
Each tiny grain of sand
Shifts a little more.

Golden-brown tints and highlights form
Giving way to tangerine
That feels so warm.
Reflections of certain silence
And the coming storm.

Sun rises higher, baking orange to white
Watching Gemini Bay
Basking in the light,
Then she shuffles off her orange
And glides towards the night.

Stephen Paul Sunter

Summer Is On Its Way

Summer is on its way
And the days are improving
Day by day by day
With landscapes filled
With glorious colour
And fields beginning to show
How they can protect their yields
Such as no other, yes summer
Is saying hello all over the lands
With its wondrous ways of showing
That we all should be thankful
To our Lord for He understands.

Colin Hush

Seaside

The feel of the sand beneath my toes
A sea breeze blowing my hair
Oh, what can compete with a summer break
By the sea in this land so fair?

The salty smell of seaweed
The mewing of gulls in the sky
The sound of the waves as they lap the shore
The sea's own lullaby.

Children's excited chatter
As they gaze in their buckets with glee
At a host of exotic small creatures
They have found in a pool by the sea.

The boats full of eager trippers
Sailing around the bay
The piers with their many attractions
To enjoy and enrich the day.

When the harsh cold of winter's upon us
My memories will warm me through
Reliving our days away, dear
Of the sun, sand, sea and you.

Shirley Brooks

Holiday

Down, down, down to the sea
Away from the cares of the world
Away, away, away we do flee
Like stones from a catapult hurled.

No time to test with trembling toe
(For so to do would be too slow)
The temperature of the ocean blue
So bidding sand and land adieu

As if in that element we were born
Our heads to the sea we do adorn
To join the other bathers there
The cool sea, the waves to share.

We bathe in nature's sea at last
Where cares are gone and worries past
And as we swim and frolic there
The finest joy on Earth we share.

And after this upon the sand
We soak the sun up something grand
Depending on our point of view
Clothes are optional for some of you.

Royston Herbert

Summer Floods

Avon, Thames, Severn and Leam
Softly gliding in the green
Land of our Midland England.
Deceivers, leading us to believe
Only in their beguiling beauty,
Dissembling with their soft fluidity
Like a woman coyly advancing
Her charm on a deluded lover,
Becoming nasty all of a sudden,
Assaulting her once-loved one
Turning from liquid lapping kisses
To a fierce overwhelming passion,
A Lucretia or a Cleopatra destined
To betray all trust and amity.
So, in this deep, desperate July
Lashed by the ubiquitous rain
These rivers betray us once again,
Uglifying landscape with brown water,
Replacing sylvan joy with slaughter
Of long-awaited summer peace.

Paul Byron Norris

Summer Reflections

A grateful peace
A world at rest,
A timeless spirit
Days blessed
With golden sunshine
And rainbow blossom,
Reflected joy
Winter forgotten:
Enjoy the moment
For it's over soon
As summer sun
Is eclipsed by a winter moon.

Arthur Pickles

Whispering Wind

Whispering through
Your hair
Yes, the wind of grace
Is surely there

Blowing the branches
Through the trees
They do sway
Silent with ease

Brushing the clouds away
To bring out the sun
We can both lay there soaking up the sun
Warmth and soothing
For everyone.

Debbie Storey

The Sun

The sun -
A flower
That
Wilts
Into a
Brown
Autumn.

Its petals
Touch
Edges
Sway
And foretell
A better
Day
Ahead.

Nicola Barnes

English Summer

The summer breeze had gently dusted round the house.
The lake shone smooth just like an antique board
that had been polished to a deep, deep sheen.
No ripple marred the surface, even fish
lay deep and somnolent, strength sapped by heat.
A single dragonfly with azure wings
flitted from reed to reed so to select
that special one down which to climb
and lay her precious eggs upon its stem.
A dandelion seed floats, so gently past
although there seems no wind to keep it up.
A slow and rhythmic creak comes from a seat
on which a man lies swinging, hat on face
and now and then the tinkling sound of ice
within a glass from which he sips to slake
his thirst and to allay the cloying heat.
The creaking slowly dies and sleep descends.
A droning wasp, drawn to the scent, comes down
and with a movement that extrudes the sting
gulps at the nectar, still cold from the ice.
As if each one had its own mobile phone
and had all been in touch, four more descend
to join their sister in the liquid feast.

Then all at once there comes a crash of sound
and in the clear blue sky, in seconds flat
appears a fiercely roiling black, black cloud.
At once the lake is cratered like the moon
as huge fat raindrops fall on it apace.
A spate of muttered curses can be heard
receding as the man runs for the house
all drowsy peacefulness now rinsed by rain
and British 'summertime' is back -
Again!

David Garde

My Old Friend

Today I found out an old friend had passed away,
A tear trickled down as I let my memories carry me away.
I remembered first meeting her, it was the middle of May,
We were looking for shade, as it was quite hot that day
And there she stood, so tall and proud,
Her cascading branches were a welcome shroud.

Every summer and every year
You would always find us sitting right here
Of course she never was alone
All the life that would make her their home
We would laugh at the squirrels as they spiralled down her thick trunk
And marvel at the magpies that hid their stolen, sparkly junk.

On a frosty morning you would stand in awe
Hundreds of beautiful spiders' webs would amaze you more.
The families she had housed year after year
Generation after generation every time would come here
And what about the great wars, one and two?
She survived them both as she grew and grew

Alas time ticks on and life carried on
It's time to sleep now, her work here is done
I sit beneath her for old times' sake
I gaze at the ground, what's this? It's no mistake
My friend has gone but she still lives on
One green shoot, the birth of her son.

I smile at this sight, no longer sad
I think of years to come and memories to be had
Of people who meet this youngster as he grows
What stories will he tell? Nobody knows
Rest in peace my wonderful friend
It is only the beginning, never the end.

Fiona Cary

Sniping At Summer

This is the season, when released
People throw clothing to the winter wind
Lift up creamy torsos to the sun
Then retire to darkened rooms
In puffed up, peeled and blistered pain.
When barbecues sulking smoke
Or flare with eyebrow-scorching flame
Sausages and burgers emerge armour-plated
And Granny's dentures cannot reach the meat.
Evenings on carefully cultivated patios
Become happy hunting grounds
For rapier-sharpened mossies,
Fruits and jams become sweet lures
For antennae of hordes of waiting wasps.
A metre of beach secured in triumph
After miles of humping burdens from the car,
Father discovers youth in digging
To the indifference of already whining kids.
Queues for loos and ice cream,
Sweat-stained collars on the office shirts,
Hordes of tourists rudely invading 'my' space,
Roads move slower than the walking feet.
Thunder rumbles and with some relief
A rush indoors is now allowed . . .
Let those who wish be outdoor macho,
For me a cooling pint within the pub.

Di Bagshawe

The Painter

God has painted the landscape
While I was asleep, last night.
Today I awoke to a picture,
A vision of pure white.

Every leaf is textured,
Carefully outlined in frost.
The fields have become a masterpiece,
Where no single detail's lost.

Even the yellow tall grass,
Which the farmer left untouched,
Has assumed an icy appearance,
Coloured by the Master's brush.

Beautiful silhouettes of trees,
Which winter rendered stark,
Resemble wonderful sculptures,
Where ice has tinted their bark.

Many dark fences and brambles,
And other things that aren't nice,
Shaded by the hand of the painter,
Have magically changed, in a trice.

From twigs and broken branches,
Down to each blade of grass,
All are detailed in brushstrokes,
And my world is transformed, as I pass.

Lorna Lea

Tunisian Sunsets

Tunisian sunset the deserts allure,
Take the hand of an angel on this day and more!
The golden door is standing ajar,
Yesterday is forgotten on this tropical shore!
Listening to nightingales in the scented night air,
Watching fireflies dance, it's as if I'm there!
Oh man in the moon, who do I love?
My past dissolves in my tingling blood!
Snakes, goats and angels are swimming to the shore,
Falling blossom like confetti is
Blown by the wind to my darling's door.
Gazing at the ocean, reflections of clouds;
Forever changing shape,
Butterflies and starfish
Fly together in the skies,
Can I stay here forever at least until I die?
Beggars and dreamers sit side by side,
The artist picks up his brush and begins to paint!

Margaret Pedley

The Sea

'The Sea', the cradle of all life
Each wave shall symbolise our strife
Each living creature she shall feed
Her children a multitudinous breed
Her colour shall reflect the sky
Sometimes she'll smile
Sometimes she'll frown
Her varied moods we shall not know why
Her friend, the sun, is smiling down.
What life shall throb beneath her waves?
Memories of heroes and of knaves
Dancing crabs and singing whales
Sharks' sharp fins with swishing tails
More colours than our minds can see
A rich treasure for you and me.

John Cook

Summer Memories

We didn't need much to be happy in days gone by
When we broke up for summer, how the days would fly
Taking it in turns to play in each one's backyard
Finding games to play was not so very hard.
We would play schools when one would be the teacher
Sums and times tables were a very big feature
Or we would put on a show, a button would be the fee
And we would each choose an act we wanted to be.
Another big favourite was hopscotch in the lane
A piece of slate and we would play time and time again
Or skipping, tying a rope end to a lamp post
Taking it in turns to wind or jump over the rope.
Playing hide-and-seek using backyard gateways
Trying to be last to be found, away from a friend's gaze
Going to the park with a picnic, sitting under a willow tree
Hiding under its branches, enjoying being free.
Or we would chalk fancy patterns on our wooden tops
Spinning them with our whips, willing them not to stop
Hula hoops, roller skates, bikes and scooters too
We were never ever short of finding things to do.

Christine Naylor

On The Beach

We were together on a beach. The sea,
Then far removed, was one of two horizons,
A ripple on the surface of our thoughts.
The sky was a complex stacking of clouds
In a gradation of colours, from blue
To grey, to green.

In that bare place
Diagrams of people played on the sand
Without conviction, each one connecting
Nothing with nothing, intimidated
By the council of the sea,
The council of the empty sea.

Stanley Downing

Idyllic Imminence

Tranquil days of summer
Occupy minds with hopeful peace
Only for a season
Then it's gone. This period has too quickly ceased.

Relaxing, midst the rocky pools
Where crabs and gulls do mingle
Are they, the seagulls, singing songs
While travelling t'ward Cave Fingal?

Gently the ocean ebbs and flows
Trees standing strong like soldiers
Kids building castles in the sand
While their pets attempt to run faster.

Such idyllic locations can be real
To some it's only a dream
The sun shines periodically
Thus brightening dreary scenes.

Yearly the pleasure of such experience
Fills life with anticipation
Lifts hope levels from daily drudge
To realms of participation.

From the moment of entry into this world
We're embarking on a journey
Many experiences we'd rather forget
But with company, we enjoy travel together.

Jesus, Saviour and friend, will traverse every day
If one desires His company
His presence within strengthens the will to sing
Of eternal bliss forever, abiding with Him.

Annie Harcus

Suffolk Summer (A Kyrielle)

If you've not seen the Suffolk skies
Nor heard the circling curlews' cries
Nor seen the swirling Sandlings blown
Then never summer have you known.

If you, in haste, eshewed the rain
That glistens in a Dunwich lane
Or haven't tramped the fen, alone
Then never summer have you known.

If you've not eyed an Ufford pew
Nor Raedwald's grave at Sutton Hoo
Nor harvested a seed that's sown
Then never summer have you known.

If you've not whiled away the hour
By Deben, Alde and Ore and Stour
Nor found a place to call your own
Then never summer have you known.

Peter Davies

Summer

Flowers' lingering fragrance
As you breathe in the warm summer air
Gentle intervalled breeze
Catches in your hair
Birds' sweet, cheerful singing
Bringing joy to your ears
Sun shining brightly
Dries up any tears
Trees adorned with green and splendour
As you wonder at this new season
Everything looks so beautiful
Everything has a reason
Look at the sky, pale velvet blue
And isn't the effect of it clever
Makes you feel so much more like living
Oh, why can't it be summer forever?

Lynda Hughes

My Special Moment

We have our special cove to watch the sunset at leisure
Mighty rocks are a backdrop in this moment of pleasure
To enhance this setting come the jewel-like stars
We wish upon a fallen one for the nights to be ours
The man in the moon's on time, bringing the light
As the acoustics of the tide play on this romantic night
This moonlit lantern reflects on the strolling sea
I find it enticing as it rolls closer to me
As I walk barefoot in the sand
With my loved one, holding his hand
The ripples of the sea gently caress our feet
We smile at each other as our eyes meet
How can I make this moment last forever?
The voice of my heart makes an endeavour
As I whisper to my love, 'Oh je t'adore.'
Knowing the tide is ebbing, leaving this shore
It's a moment in time you never want to end
As an exciting shiver through your bodies extends
Soulmates unite and make a heartfelt declaration
Writing their names in the sand full of elation
Oh, to make the sun, moon and stars stand still
As our hearts make an imprint of this magical thrill
A new dawn breaks, these moments pass away
I have my special moment to remember every day.

Barbara Jermyn

Black Money

Across vast plains - mountain ranges
And rainforest - a river meanders through
A far-off land and a far-off place
Unknown to the group stood looking
But known very well by his ancestors
The valley below - where he lived
The river below - where he swam and fished
The endless sky above - and all this is
What he would have seen - it's unchanged
Landscape was the last he saw
Taken by canoe with others by force - then
To nearby ports sixty miles away along
Hot, dusty tracks - never to return
To a life of slavery - a plantation worker
Thousands of miles away - branded like
An animal and sold as a number in a ledger
This journey was brought about by a local college
Project tracing the slave triangle
And as they stood and looked in silence
Two hundred years of history were finally closed
And as the old man took his son's arm
Said, 'This is your homeland, your heritage'
He, in turn, looked at his son in his arms
And promised one day he would return -
And show his grandson the homeland and the price it cost.

David Charles

Holiday Shangri-La

All 'mod cons' the brochure read,
To make a booking, off Mum sped,
She reserved a caravan
Big enough for all our clan,
A six-berth, close to the wood,
On a hill, it sounded good.
So, off to Clacton we did trot
In hired van that stunk of grot!
On the journey I was sick,
Chucking up on brother Mick,
Then at last our camp we sighted,
Dad paid the driver, we alighted,
'Shangri-La' the place was called
But how that name had our mum fooled,
We clambered up a hilly track,
Through the bracken we did hack,
We found our van, it weren't too grim,
Well, after Mum had hit the Vim;
But we never knew what lay in store,
There were shocks by the score!
Still, we tried to enjoy our stay
But of 'mod cons' I've this to say,
'Modern washroom' yeah, for sure!
Wooden mangle by the door!
Roaches crawled around the drains,
Rushing blood through my veins,
Showers were broken, toilets were blocked
And in the eaves sparrows flocked!
As for the ground within the park
There were no lights when it went dark!
We had to hope the moon was bright
So we could walk around at night.
'Swimming pool with fountain flowing',
Nope! Empty pond with weeds a-growing!

'Little green with children's dell',
Was it there? Was it Hell!
There were tyre swings on rusty frames,
A worn dirt patch for playing games
And when it rained the place did flood,
The road was lost, it turned to mud.
So, off Mum went to enquire
Why the place was so dire.
She was told they were having probs
Getting round to all those jobs.

But we decided 'What the heck!'
And to the beach we did trek;
The campsite bus we waited for
Unaware what lay in store,
Old Routemaster red and rusted
Windows cracked and seats all busted!
But the final shock was still to come,
You should have seen the look on Mum!
As in the cab the driver dived
For of one arm he was deprived!
He swung that bus from left to right,
To keep our seats we held on tight!
We used that bus throughout our stay,
Mum went rigid, Dad turned grey!
Two weeks passed and home we went,
To return we'd no intent.
But, as time passed by, we reflected
On the memories we'd collected,
The following year we didn't go far,
Yes, we went back to Shangri-La!

Pauline Jones

Summer Fête

Children's excited laughter and delight
Such a wonderful day, so sunny and bright
Silver town band setting the scene
Aunt Elsie rather large for the small trampoline.

Sideshows, a juggler, Punch and Judy
Sword-swallower, fire-eater, we can be choosy
Face-painted children like the cast of 'Cats'
Helter-skelter kids whizzing down on their mats.

The vicar's dancing to the music of the band
Seen supping in the beer tent, could be half-canned
Hot dog stand with relish or onions
Poor Mrs Martin resting her bunions.

Popcorn, candyfloss, ice cream cornets
The buzz of the crowd like so many hornets
Screams of delight at 'Tip Aunt Sally Out Of Bed'
With so many tumbles, Sally's poor bottom must be red.

PA system announcing raffles and attractions
A little girl lost in all these distractions
The fortune teller's tent with her crystal ball
But it's old Mrs Jones, not a gypsy at all!

The raffle's been drawn with dozens of winners
It's time to go home to takeaway dinners
Everyone still - the band's playing 'The Queen'
Undoubtedly, the best fête the town's ever seen.

The children will remember this day forever
So it was worth everyone's unstinting endeavour
These children in a possible far-distant date
Will be taking their children to a grand summer's fête.

Len Peach

The Sun-Worshippers

It's that time of year again
The 'darling buds of May' have blossomed
Lured like Icarus, towards the sun
Warming up, after a cold winter.

Car parks cram-packed, fit to burst
The sun-worshippers have arrived, en masse
Children are leaping in all directions
Fathers stagger, weighed down beasts of burden.

Grandpa curses at the radio
England must have lost another wicket
Footballs and kites flying all around
Punch and Judy holding centre stage.

Buckets and spades for the sandcastle army
Futile attempts to hold back the tide
Inflatables and surfboards hunting down the swimmers
Ice creams and worries melting fast.

Red lobsters plonk down on straining deckchairs
A tattoo land, body-pierced, motley crew
Spitting, swearing, smoking and drinking
And that's just the children.

A 'Turner' sky appears right out of the blue
'I told you we should have gone to Spain.'
The nation of experienced, trained athletes
Pack up and sprint towards their cars.

The car park attendant, left all alone
To fiddle the takings before the boss man comes
A sea of litter to be cleared away
By a dreary patrol, before tomorrow's invasion.

John Green

Summer Oasis

Sitting in the garden whiling away my time
Thoughts and memories in the lovely warm sunshine.

The aroma of the flowers, greenery swaying in the gentle breeze
A dog barking, a blackbird singing in the trees.

Calmness in a life of hurry, scurry, doing this and that
In contemplation, while stroking the snoring cat.

The busy bee fastidious in his work
A vapour trail in the blue, above the meadow a hovering hawk.

An English country scene? Perhaps a dreamer's fantasy?
Forgetting life's worries of practicalities and reality?

Plants and flowers, unlike us they bloom, fade and die
Dormant in wintry months until once more they peer into the sky.

We live our span and fear our eventual demise
Seeing life and death in nature's fall and rise.

A tingle up my spine of why we are here
To live and die, then to live again, I dwelt on that and drained my beer.

George Carrick

The Seaside

Hear the laughter of children
Running about on the sand,
Listen to the sound of music,
The trumpets playing in the band.

Boats with brightly coloured sails,
Sunbathers with wide-brimmed hats
Sipping ice-cold drinks
Late into the night.

As night falls
The revellers stagger home,
Leaving the beach littered with debris,
Seagulls devouring left-over crumbs.

Cathy Mearman

Summer On The Beach

Oh, it is the season of summer
When we think of the beach
And the bronzed lithe bodies
So they think
Except now the bodies have swollen with good living
To be bronzed but not lithe anymore
But sporting the rolls of fat
That speak of twenty-first century plague
As rolls of fat spill out from legs under swimsuits
Or spill over bathing costumes
That were once several sizes too small
But now are replete
With sated girth
Oh, how the myth was made!
And the papers spill out
Perfect people
Lithe and thin in every way
Without thinking of that twenty-first century plague
Of the sedentary lifestyles
And the obesity epidemic.

Alasdair Sclater

Early Summer

Although it's only April
The weather is so warm
The sun comes out early
Which is not the usual norm
We all enjoy the weather
It's so pleasant in the sun
It's early for the deckchairs
But that's how it should be done
It's great to have an early start
To this lovely weather
I am sure it will carry on
And we'll get tanned together.

Mary Tickle

Summer Reflections

The temperature's rising
But that's not surprising
The sun is high in the sky
It's midsummer season
And that is the reason
Why gardens are dusty and dry.

Road tarmac is melting
Everyone's sweltering
There's bare flesh and knobbly knees
Not one cloud to be seen
A sun-worshipper's dream
Ice cream and strawberry teas.

But, come next December
So few will remember
Those sizzling days of July
Because they'll be freezing
And coughing and sneezing
Under a dark wintry sky.

Brian Wood

Sunny Honey

Waves lap gently over
Sandy shore so white -
While we feel the sun
Gently warm our skin.

This is our paradise
Where the summer is an eternity.
It has a beginning
There is no end . . .

Our secret paradise has a place
In our hearts.
Gives us so much bliss . . .
It can't get any better than this!

Jagdeesh Sokhal

To A Newt

I found a newt in a dying pond
A pretty little one, drying out
In mud, caked, half-buried
From a former sighing life.

Only her eyes told me she was yet alive
Pleading at me
Long narrowing beads
Gasping to be free from that baking death.

Gently, I cradled her in my hands
Lifting her, I put her in a jar
Watched her shuffle back to life
Struggling with dehydrated limbs;
Wriggling off the caked, filthy, cloying past
Of longing sticks
And lying autumnal leaves

She looked at me with fearful eyes -
The Magdalene's eyes of salvation -
Smiling she mouthed her 'Raboni!'
I knew I had to let her go
To let her live.

I freed her in my friend's pond
And watched her swim
In cleansing joy and hope
And pirouette among the lilies of faith.

Often I'll sit by that pond
And watch my newt
Enjoying life
The life she was meant to have
Knowing that she's safe and well.

Ian Burnett

Floods

Rain, rain go away
Please don't come back another day
Water; water everywhere and not a drop to drink
These old sayings make you think
Please flood, go away from our door
You visited us before
Seeing our living room a-stream
How I wish it were all a bad dream
People and animals suffering
Wondering what tomorrow will bring?
Please God, don't let it rain
All we want is to get back to normal again
We're at our wits' end
It's driving us round the bend
Now gone is the flood
Leaving behind sewage and mud
God, if this is global warming
Please can't You give us some warning?

Richard Trowbridge

Spring

Spring is dancing through town again,
her magic warrant makes all green,
'Wake up you dreamers!' hear the fairy call,
'gone is the snow, gone is the snow!'
Stretching their heads sleepily,
are crocus and lily of the valley,
apple and cherry blossom's splendour
they make spring such a wonder,
heavenly perfumes fill the air
and say that spring is here.
The birds are back from holidays,
warm and soft the sun's rays,
listen to the happy songs
of starlings feeding their young.

Sybille Krivenko

Summer Magic

The teasing British summer hides and waits
Increases yearning thoughts of summers past
Throws sunbeams here or there, then hesitates
Until one day decides to stay at last.

The British summer like a changeling child
Sometimes with rain will increase river flow
Then smile and bring a spell of weather mild
Is inconsistent, strange and hard to know.

Our summer season is a mystery
A golden fairy with a wealth to share
A wayward elemental in our destiny
Yet we are always glad when summer's there.

Come sunlight, moonlight, fantasy and verse
Come Andrew Lang, Hans Anderson and Tolkein
Take us beyond grim prophecies and worse
To where wishes are granted in-between.

Kathleen Mary Scatchard

My Garden In May

Our garden in May always looks pleasant.
With hawthorn buds,
that bloom into pretty petals.
The warmth and tranquillity in light evenings and day.
Soft gentle rain.
Dogs go for a walk, on leash and with snacks.
They welcome the weather.
The sun and rain's warmth freshens the hair on their backs.
An American silver tabby - slender, sleek cat.
Daisies greet the sunshine.
Close clasped tightly for the night.
An occasional dandy.
Then there's more in sight.
This garden welcomes all, but shame on those who disrespect it,
and make misery for us all.

Rachel Van Den Bergen

San Gimignano

I see them still -

Fourteen towers
five centuries tall
challenging the Tuscan sky
above slopes of cypress
and sun-filled fruit
bowing the vines.

In cloisters dressed
with faded frescos
we dream to cool pure notes
from a busker's flute
or tap our feet
to staccato guitar.

Dusk dims the radiance
of the piazza
the silken air is threaded
with beads of operatic
voices rehearsing
on the Duomo steps.

I hear them still.

Maggie Andrews

Heatwave

Under the yew tree
Dusty behind wire mesh,
Black-eared, black back,
In wooden hutch,
Bugs closes beady eye
And puffs white chest.

Sunshine on the lawn
Shaded by the yew.
A chaffinch on the roof
Trills through wisteria.
Grass skirts of willow,
Orange lily and fuschia.

Pink tints of phlox,
Honeysuckle, peach and red
And night-scented stocks
Emulsion the flower bed.
Frozen in attitudes of dance,
Petals blooming,
Roses get a second chance
To arabesque before pruning.

Rosemary Benzing

Untitled

Beyond the branches and the treetops - lies another world
Far distant from this one I have come to love and know.
For here my world is sheltered - is filled with calm and peacefulness,
From here - I never really - want to go.
What draws me to this place are sounds of nature -
From every bush and every tree and in every scene.
Along the riverbanks - the holes and crevices - and
So much more - that in my lifetime - I shall never see!
And friends - people whom I've never known before
Sharing this same love and tranquillity.
It seems like Heaven - has opened its doors
To the ordinary folk, like you and me.
And in the morning - when the dew lays on the ground
And the sun begins to rise - the richness of the warmth spills over me.
The glistening - rippling waters - licking gently at the banks -
The beauty almost hurts my eyes to see.
On through the day I hear the whispering of the trees
As they gently air their leaves and see the bird life - oh so busy
                                                on the wing.
Then once their tasks are all accomplished, I hear the rustle
                                                in the bushes
Where they find a branch to preen themselves and - sing.
How glorious - their activities and devotion to the day!
As evening begins to move right in, the sun goes down and rests -
                                                behind the world
And who should appear? Moon - rising high - seeming to wear a grin.
Then almost silence - the night is still,
I close the blinds but take a peep outside. Moon is shining
                                                on the waters,
No clouds - so she can't roll away and hide.
I catch this moment in my heart - I do not want to miss a thing -
I do not want to shut the night away
But - long before I know it - I am fast asleep and then awaken -
To a brand new day.

Tomboy

Wet, Wet, Wet Wetland . . .

Chirp-chirrup, caw or squawk, but above all, quack
Because you can see Wetland come back.

To any migrating flock pass on our word
Tell them what, on flood-plains, has occurred
Where once those humans in their traffic jams stuck
Thoroughfares widen for goose and duck.
Though an elegant swan may swim down the street
A glistening lake is drowning the wheat.
It's as if the sky against Earth held some grudge
And longed to turn all land into sludge
But then decided to cover up that mud
Whereupon a deluge caused this flood.
Not a summer to universally please -
Certainly not, butterflies and bees -
Or humans up to necks or, at least, their knees
Though able to row small boats with ease.
Even to travel like us, some of them try -
Clumsy helicopters in the sky
Whose pilots can see where riverbanks gave way
And where rising waters still hold sway.
The occasional green island may appear -
Bedraggled cattle try to reach here -
Fish are swimming where they never swam before
Past many a sandbagged bank or door.
For all fish-eating birds a possible treat -
Stranded fish when the waters retreat.
So in this unusual summer weather
Feathered fish-eaters, *flock together!*

Chirp-chirrup, caw or squawk, above all, quack
Because you have seen Wetland come back.

Chris Creedon

Diamanté; A South American Dream

The diamond faerie in autumn's fire
her silken locks set the downs ablaze
in cascading flames that softly glow
in the songs sung in the light of autumn's rays.

Yet summer Diamanté sparkles blue
such jewels, prisms reflect in her smiling eyes
mystic pools, two sparkling diamond hue
so clear, charismatic and bright.

Diamanté takes our breath away
silhouetting in the candlelight
and we are entranced, by her radiance
gasping in this beauty shining bright.

An enchanting nymph so lovely
lulls us into peaceful dream.
Born surely in the faerie kingdom
Diamanté, our faerie queen.

Ann Hubbard

Enchanting Butterfly

Butterfly, your wings are beautifully made
You're like a fairy fluttering in a fairy glade
You love the colourful flowers so eye-catching
All mix and matching
You flutter in the warm sunny haze
In summer's fly-away days
You enchant, captivate, fascinate
You flutter with the dragonfly
Your relation, your playmate
You say hello to your country companions
Along the way
Remembering the dreams of yesterday
You flutter in the warmth of the sun
Having so much fun
You flutter your soft satin wings of violet blue
As summer's breeze guides you through.

Joanna Maria John

This Summer

Wet and lingering, this summer rain
Splashes over cement terrain
Where are the fields of yesteryear
That would absorb Nature's tear?

Flooding, drowning, frightened fur
Scrabbling round in flapping blur
Buildings, homes sinking fast
As the rain decides to last and last.

Sodden branches on downcast trees
Water flows with apparent ease
Shivering animals crying out,
'What is this wet all about?'

Resilient Man survives the rain
Although his heart is filled with pain
As the cloak of wet decides to stay
And drive his shelters all away.

Linda Hurdwell

The Violent Storm

O, violent storm
How powerful you are!
What can I do to calm you down?
I saw you battering sea walls
And barriers down.
With heavy winds and ocean tides
O, vibrant storm,
How powerful you are!
What can I do? What can I do
To calm you down?
I saw you, blowing down houses and trees
All along your paths.
O violent storm, violent storm
How powerful you are!
What can I do? What can I do
To calm you down?

PB James

It's The Summertime Once Again

It was nine o'clock in the morning
The sun shone through my curtains
As I awoke from my beautiful sleep
To hear the birds singing upon the rooftops
Just outside my bedroom window
I got up out of bed and put on my Sunday best
And went for a stroll around the big park.

The trees looked so vibrant, lush and green
And the sky was an ocean-blue
Little whispers of white clouds floated on by
The flowers of such multitudinal colours
Huddled together, covering the land
Like a multicoloured blanket that laid upon my bed
As the sweet fragrance filled the air like perfume.

Butterflies gathered together and danced
Wild, happy and free in the summer's air
Making a wonderful display of patterns
In the ocean-blue sky
In the summertime.

As I walked around in the park
Feeling lovely and warm
I looked up at the trees
They seemed to come alive with birds
I saw blue tits and bullfinches, robins, chaffinches
Greenfinches and little common house sparrows
Flittering and chattering to and fro.

Oh, what a wonderful sight to see
While rabbits scurried through the thick, tall, rich, green grass
As bluebells seemed to dance and sway in the gentle
                              summer's breeze.

Oh, how I love the summertime
The wildlife, because everything seems so picturesque
From the tallest trees to the smallest river.

Oh, how I love summer
To sit here feeling happy and contented and free.

Samantha Rose Whitworth

Nature's Patterns

Damp leaves trodden underfoot
Dank earthy smell of rain-sodden paths
The muffled sound of distant church bells -
Was that sheep I could hear?

Silence. Yet something stirs -
Is it the wind moaning?
Hidden, yet elusively there
Darkening sky - a distant flash of
Lightning, the electrically charged air
Wanton, not knowing where or when to strike.

Suddenly - rain - beating down, slanting sideways
Stinging the face -
Birds quiet, yet stirring -
Torrent - the river, chatter loud, stones overbent.

Stars - shuddering with purple apoplexy
Visibly impaired
Tall trees bent
To the will of the wind - agonised.

Morning calm, destruction noted
Chaos, where once was none -
Work now follows -
Sadness where
Brute force of Nature
Overcomes.

Laissez-faire
Of hapless habitants
Homes hopelessly hovelled
Where Nature has been

Sweet the saviour of soul-saved days
Now to remember Heaven's heavenly ways.

Valma June Streatfield

The Hot Nevada Sun

Burning, churning
Twist and turning
Tumbleweed
A whirling, twirling
In the hot
Nevada sun
Today the Shaman's
Spell is spun
Hoping, praying
We survive
To catch the wind
And stay alive
To see our children
Grow and grow
Forever in our
Heart and soul
Laughing, crying
Young and free
A prayer for
All humanity.

Rod Trott

In The Spring

I smell sweet-scented flowers
That all around my garden grow
And I admire them for hours
Such a beautiful multicoloured show

In early spring there are the daffodils
And primroses beneath my window sills
And all kinds of flowers around the lawn
To scatter their scents from early dawn

There are brightly coloured tulips
In many lovely pastel shades
To spread sweet-scented fragrances
Before the sunlight dims and fades.

A V Carlin

The Lonely Duck

I saw a duck
By the pond today
He seemed to be there
To stay.

I hadn't noticed
Him there before
Sifting for food
On the muddy shore.

He looked lonely
Paddling there on the brink
A mallard duck
Having a drink.

The sunshine shone
On his plumage gay
Then he spread his wings
And flew away.

Dorothy Foster

Bluebell Wood At Brockweir

Delicate, trembling shades of blue
Blending to a distant view,
Lapping round the silver trees
With green-leaved spears all sparkling in the breeze.
A million bluebells carpeting the ground -
What better sight in springtime to be found?
Honey-scented,
Well presented,
Bluebells standing calm and still,
A picture painted on a sloping hill.
And then, a sudden breeze across the coloured ground -
What shimmering pleasure can there be found?

Eileen M Lodge

Summer Days

Summer months are nearly here,
Warmth and brightness, best time of year.
Pretty flowers all in bloom,
Bursts of sunshine fill the room.

Long, warm, balmy days,
Reflecting the beautiful summer's rays.
We get our fair share of rain,
But the brilliance is soon back again.

You can lie on the grass,
Overhead, white fluffy clouds will pass.
Sunshine gets into your eyes,
Hiding the brilliance of the azure skies.

And as you sit or lie,
The bees buzz as they go by.
Butterflies flutter past, seems the sky is alive,
With all the birds that twitter, sing and dive.

Holidays not far away,
The sun invites us out to play.
The countryside is in full bloom,
Summer sounds are a joyful tune.

Long may the sun upon us shine,
Then we'll have a happy time.
An abundance of good things to enjoy,
Nature's own, wonderful ploy.

Olive Young

The Fish

Perpetual curving, hollow whorls
Shape to shape moving against current;
Curved world
Universally wide drifts into darkness.
A flash of light above
Darting fire breams;
Silent waters weave mysterious cloth
About him, eternal shiftings
Tides ebb/flow washing foamy lace
That crashes above, dark fire leaps
In his blood, wind calls, he rises
Sees bright stars glittering
Darkness gathers him up and
Slips into his being
He rises towards light
Then sinks again into dark void
Secrets whispering through waters
Rhythm throbs in his temples
Moving, gliding, twisting to a
Musical flow, he darts again towards
Light: up and up, over first hurdle
Rushing torrent casts him back, up rocky
Stair and into freedom; swiftly
Wriggling against current towards call
That is so strong - pain! Sharpness
Along his back, quick, no air to breathe
Eyes dull, mouth stills. Otter feeds.

Teresa Webster

Enchanted

Walking amongst woodland, trees and ferns
Morning dew arising
Silent deer wandering by
There is no sound
Too early for birds in the sky
Take in the earthy smell
The scent of mud and leaves
Summertime is here at last
It is 24 hours of fun.

Mellow breeze and salty air
Fill my body with sea
Relaxed and happy, content just to be
Lying tanning in the sun
Coconut oil and sea spray wash over my body
And cleanse my soul
For hours I could stay.

Camp fire aglow in the garden
Watching stars twinkle in the sky
No street lights or cars racing
Warm night air and insect cry
Another long summer's day over
I close my eyes and drift gently asleep
Under a midnight-blue Heaven.

Jane Cooter

Summer Days

I remember lazy summer days
The calmness of the breezeless haze
Smelling fresh-cut grass
Millpond like mirrored glass
Warm, sedate summer dream
Of tea, strawberries and cream
Cricket played upon the village green
How I picture that scene
In the distance on the horizon grey clouds loom
To faraway echoes of rumbling thunder's boom
Dark clouds hang aloft
Deluged fields and orchards croft
She, the tempest, raises her head
Causing panic and confusion's dread
Lightning strikes to and from the ground
To the vibrating of thunder's sound
The storm gathering to an exciting peak
Electric air in static does speak
As the torrent subsides
Distant dark clouds run away and hides
Now the shy sun peeks out and birds start to sing
To the freshness after a storm does bring
People return to those normal days
I remember lazy summer days.

Terry Powell

Other Worlds - Other Lives

Hear the crickets' curious rasp
Secreted in the summer grass
Slumberous drone of a bee
Pollen hunting busily
See ant and earwig scurry round
On urgent missions bound
Snails' slow, deliberate progress
Border bound, intent on plant distress
Woodlice armies swift recoil
To safety in a damp wood pile
Compare butterflies' erratic dance
With a dragonfly's direct advance.

As night replaces day
Others emerge, their roles to play
Observe a moth's frenetic flight
Drawn irresistibly to light
Midges dancing in a cloud
Buzzing echoes sound so loud
Fluorescent spotlights dot the grass
As female glow-worms pleasure ask
The insects' world unseen, unknown
Diverse and complex as our own.

Sue Cann

Where Peace And Love Abides

A butterfly - so beautiful
Rested upon my hand
Bathed lazily in sunshine
Perfection - godly planned.

Coloured wings of rainbows
Shimmered in the sun
A few more days of living
Then beauty would be done.

Light breezes then passed over
Encouraged flight to wings
Then fluttered into my arbour
A 'present' - fit for kings.

A butterfly - so beautiful
Rested upon my hand
A moment of perfection
Amid a much tormented land.

A butterfly - so beautiful
In 'golden light' now flies
Was tended by its Master
Where peace and love abides.

Maureen Westwood O'Hara

Wild-Fowlers Call The Fens Their Own

Walking on stilts when waters rise
In peat-black land, with interludes
Of sedges and reeds; they view wide skies
Which exhibit all Norfolk's moods.

A busy dinghy makes liquid
Sounds as it shifts water along
In back streams, round the reed-fronded
Eyots - promising warblers' song.

Behind an islet, who knows what
Kinds of unwary duck or goose
Swims, or sits in a brooding squat
On eggs, for its last moments loose?

Its death-cause lies beside the oars
Employed by fellows, whose one thought
Is to bring a mortal pause
To poultry their wives might have bought!

Gillian Fisher

Skyline

The blazing sun hides behind the frosty cloud of sky, piercing through,
Whilst the burning orange skyline disintegrates
And the waves crash against the promenade;
Leaving a spray of mist behind -
As I'm taken back, to all those years ahead of me.
I cannot see the sounds that the neon lights produce when refracting
                                                    off the sea,
But I can feel the summer sun setting upon the hazy horizon.
The glassy waves wash away, emotionlessly, the
                              white-powdered sands
And what's left of the colour in the sky is captivated by the night.
The summer sky is dying; the winter warmth is rising.

Melissa Brabanski

Adventurers' Fen

Drizzle dulls the early summer evening.
Here, where there is the sound of no sound,
The sweet sound of silence fills the senses.

As the wind whispers, mourning in the reeds,
Birdsong clears the mind, while memories
Speak of days past, days lost.

Suddenly a barn owl swoops,
Quartering his territory, searching
Silently for survival. He hovers,
Then plummets, feet first to the ground,
Before rising - a small mammal swinging
From his sharp talons. He heads for home.
A life given for a life.

As the white ghost of heartache searches
For lost love. Held here, safe in the sound of no sound,
Stays the lost sound of silence, pure and clear;
Giving the soft stillness the blessing of peace.

Anita Richards

God Of All Creation

God of all creation
We bow before You in adoration
You give us sunshine and showers, flowers and trees
Mountains and valleys, You made all of these
The sunrise and sunset are beautiful to see   '
God created these things for you and me
So with hearts full of love, we stand up and say
Thank You Lord for each new day.

Wendy Calow

Spring's Glory

May Day you have come our way
Now the light shines so bright
As the sun shines its light
Everyone is on the go
Now it's time for a new start
Nature will play its part
The joy all over the land
Flowers blow in the breeze
Perfume is everywhere
Roses burst into bloom
Red, yellow, pink ones too
Beauty is here to see
An everlasting memory
So open, so free
Like the birds in the tree
Blackbirds, sparrows, robins too
A magic land for us to view
A love that shines for you.

Gordon Forbes

Sunrise

I am the sunrise
See me shine
On all around
My light sublime;
How the darkness
Shrinks, far away
As I announce
The beginning of the day:
'At last it has begun
My kingdom has come!'

Trevor De Luca

The Floods; Summer 2007

As many rivers flood
Roads become oceans of mud
Cars and homes become submerged
As the water levels have surged
Reservoirs can't hold
All the water, we're told
So it must be pumped out
As we recover from 'drought'
As you wade in the dark
The message is stark
It's time to build an ark
If you want dry lands
Move to the highlands
As now the lowlands
Are no-go lands
The north winds blow
Where did summer go?

Catherine Blackett

Springtime On Shipbourne Common

Part of me is beyond the view
As I stand on this hillside
With everything new!
Glorious season, all nature abounds.
A deep inner peace,
Benediction profound!
Then, there's a pause,
When silence takes over
Surrounded by wild flowers,
And a four-leaf clover!
Savour this moment, alas, it cannot last,
File it in the memory, a cameo of the past.

Betty Willeard

All For Free

In the autumn of your life
When you have some time to spare
Look at the world around you
Nature's gifts are everywhere.

Like the waves on the shore
That break with a thunderous roar
The birds in the sky that glide and soar
The first snowdrops that appear through the hardened soil
Worms that emerge through the earth as they twist and uncoil
The fluorescent trail left by a snail gleaming on the metal rail
The complicated cobweb suspended as if by a nail
Birds nesting, what a joy to behold
Collecting, gathering their eggs to enfold.

The damp grass glistening after a recent shower
Globules of water adhering to the blades that glow with
                                    technicolor power
Clouds drifting, displaying a touch of blue
Then a shaft of light descends, a promise of warmth to renew
Squirrels scampering up a tree
The colourful sight of a bumblebee.

This visual bliss
A never-ending abyss.

Gloria Hargreaves

Buttercups And Daisies

My lawn is strewn with buttercups and daisies,
Their petals open when the sun comes up,
They prettily enhance the lawn with white and yellow specks,
At sunset their petals all fold up.

I can't see why some people think they're weeds,
They gave my daughter many happy hours,
Picking them and making them into a floral chain,
Nobody's lawn is prettier than ours.

When the lawn is mowed, it makes the garden all smell nice,
But all the little flowers lose their heads,
Perhaps it would be better if we got lawn-flower seeds,
And sowed them into bordering flower beds.

It doesn't really take too long before they all revive,
And show their pretty flower heads once more,
Our buttercups and daisies are such hardy little plants,
They're never missing too long, that's for sure.

Without these white and yellow splodges peppering the lawn,
The lawn would be a solid mass of green,
The prettiness of little flowers set into the grass
Gives us delight, the best we've ever seen.

Mick Nash

Come Spring

Come spring; and bring an end to winter's night!
'Tis with joy I'll shed my cold weather coat,
From first bud to last flower, a clear delight!

Returning birds do flock in carefree flight,
Mating mallards avoid the angler's float,
Come spring; And bring an end to winter's night!

Crocuses peep through the soil in clusters tight,
The newborn lambs are gambolling with a goat,
From first bud to last flower, a clear delight!

In nests the birds add padding soft and light,
Upon the lake once more I spy a boat,
Come spring; and bring an end to winter's night!

The winter stoat's fur turns to brown from white,
While daffodils ring round a filling moat,
From first bud to last flower, a clear delight!

Look round, the sun-kissed land, from left to right,
At Mother Nature's prize, I smugly gloat,
Come spring; and bring an end to winter's night!
From first bud to last flower, a clear delight!

Linda Coleman

The Coming Of Winter

Winter is upon us, dark clouds are in the sky
The birds are all migrating; I look up and watch them fly.

Trees are shedding off their leaves, all strewn around the ground
Squirrels storing all their nuts, knowing where they can be found.

Hedgehogs rolling into balls, it's hibernation time
I don't think they'll wake up again, until the weather's fine.

A tortoise walks across the leaves, he's very slow and sleepy
He's looking for somewhere to hide, it's all so quiet and creepy.

Plants die off and drop their blooms, but the roots they stay alive
Until the sun returns again, then they'll grow and thrive.

The wildlife grow their thick fur coats, to keep them nice and warm
They'll need them soon, as the wind picks up, here comes
another storm.

A rabbit hides down in his burrow, until the storm has passed
Then out to find some dandelions, which he gobbles down quite fast.

The snow it settles all around, no wildlife to be seen
Until the spring is back again and everything is green.

Olive White

Summer's Flight

Thunder quakes
Lightning forks
Fresh scent of rain.

Summer storms
In humid heat
Soft harvests grain.

Trees fulfilled
Fruit matured
Late roses grow.

Flowers fade
Long days decrease
New changes blow.

All Earth moves
In space unplaced
The galaxy bright.

Waning sun
Grey cloudy skies
Comes winter's night.

Maureen Plenderleith

Springtime

Spring heralds a new dawn,
Sleeping earth awakes.
Long-gone are the winter nights,
With their gently falling flakes.
Fragrances mingle on the breeze,
Of bluebells and daffodils.
Spring is fully upon us,
To cure our winter ills.
Winds blow away the chills,
As robins and blackbirds sing.
A bright new cheery season,
Is now in full swing.

Donna Salisbury

My Golden Champa Tree

How tall and straight
grew my Champa tree

scent inebriating
my home, my garden

my bower of terracotta
flowerpots, old teapots

discarded cooking pots
anything that could

hold up roots
How my tree gave

its shade and fragrance
to all, to the geckoes

on my walls, misplaced
sparrows, crows

any friend passing
by, they were all canopied.

How I wish now
for its scent, sealed

in a glass vial
perhaps, to inhale

every time
the dust and grime

clog up my nose
and numb my mind

petrifying all fine
feelings within.

Rumjhum Biswas

Spring Has Sprung

Spring has sprung or so they say
It can be hard to know
When blooms that should come out in May
Appeared two months ago

Despite all that it must be said
Springtime is rather fine
With longer days and shorter nights
When you start to see the signs

Of renewed growth, awakening trees
Birds and bees coming out to play
Revelling in some new-found warmth
At the start of every day

Warm days, however, are not all
New smells the season brings
Fresh-cut grass, young blooms in flower
Also welcome in the spring

Despite the fact that spring's approach
Is not predictable as years gone past
With climate changing all the time
We know we can at last

Acknowledge its arrival
With hearts no longer hardened
By lack of warmth and nights too long
And evenings in pub gardens

So hooray, I say, for spring has sprung
It even managed to be kind
Enough to encourage lazy me
To compose this little rhyme.

Claire Rushbrook

Down In Our Wood

Down in our wood
Where the trees grow so tall
All the autumn leaves
Are beginning to fall
They drift to the ground
Like soft drifting flakes
As a scattered carpet
Of autumn it makes
As the green turns to
Orange and yellow and red
The tree branches droop
As if ready for bed
All the ivy that's wrapped
Round the trunks of the trees
Grips on so tightly
Strong in the breeze
There's a stream trickling by
At a nice steady pace
Nothing round here
Seems to be in a race
I look round in awe
At the sights all around
Oh and there goes a frog
As he croaks out his sound
There's much more to see
For nature's so good
So I look forward till next time
I walk in our wood.

Sheila High

Haute Marne

The greening curve of the canal
Beckons us on, through locks and villages
Through towns
The countryside unfolds
Majestic in its beauty and peaceful
With its fields of ripening corn
With trees reflected in the water
Their mirror-images are broken by our passing
Then settle back in soft tranquillity
A heron rises from the bank-side reeds
Our silent passage does not cause him much distress
He joins the kites and buzzards overhead
Then comes to rest again
Where sandpipers at the water's edge
Repeat their trilled refrain
Though we must soon forsake these wondrous things
We shall take with us and distil for future use
The memories of happy days
Spent cruising the canal.

Christina Stowell

Spring

The yellow carpets of daffodils
And blue of the bluebells
The delicate flower of the primrose
Are all signs of spring.
As trees reveal their green
And buds appear we know
Spring isn't far away.
Let us thank the Lord that winter is passing
And spring is on its way.
Sometimes the rain is heavy
Sometimes it's very light
It is sent to help the flowers
Show us their beauty in the spring.

Jean Martin-Doyle

A Delightful Cycle Ride

My cycle is coloured orange and green
What beautiful countryside we have seen
We travel along the Forest Way
A true delight I really must say.

This is a track where steam trains once ran
With all their splendour and so grand
Now it is a haven for wildlife you see
With fox and rabbit and badger to name three.

But a place where horse riders, walkers and cyclists can go
Winter, the trees look like fairyland with the sparkling frost and snow
Spring, with buds bursting and new green leaves of the trees
Birds in the hedges, busy nest-building in the warm breeze.

Summer, pass fields of yellow oil-seed rape and golden corn
Fields of sheep looking so forlorn
Buttercups, meadowsweet and foxgloves so tall
Then acorns, conkers and coloured toadstools.

Anne Churchward

Springtime

I love the springtime of the year
In the gardens the first flowers appear,
Aconites, snowdrops, brave the cold
What a joy they are to behold.
Later, the daffodils will bloom
Nodding golden heads to the breezy tune.
Tulips will follow, in colours gay
Brightening up a cold dull day.
The freshness of spring brings so much cheer
It really is the best time of the year.

Vera Hankins

To English Hills Baptised In Eden

The fabled Sphinx still stares, transfixed
Across the burning desert sands
To English hills baptised in Eden
Where tall trees like living statues
Watch through the windless day
Like millions of scattered diamonds
The morning dew reflects the sun
Silken webs, spider's thread
White cotton wool-clouds drift
Across the patchwork fields
Casting fleeting, rolling shadows
Beneath the sapphire-blue domed sky
Fluffy balls of dandelion seeds
Rise, dance upon the air
Sycamore seeds spin and spiral
Seraph sylph-like fairies
With wings of shimmering mother of pearl
Live in the dreams of children and of men
Silver showers sweep across the plain
Evaporate in summer's heat
The sweet aroma of the rose
Mingles with the smell of freshly cut grass
A Sumerian sunset stuns the senses
And Babylon would find a bride
In lush green English gardens
Night descends, steals the rainbow's day
The rising full moon the lovers' orb
Paints the land a silvery ghostly grey
And the stars are bright on Orion's Belt
That watched the passing of the day.

David Walford

Crystal Morn

Sometimes on a crystal morn
I wake up early to greet the dawn
Shades of amber fill the sky
As the sun starts rising high
Then the clouds all fluffy and bright
Break the amber and blue with shards of white.

If I watch the sky at dusk
The sky turns reddish-brown like rust
As the burning sun sets low
With shades of red and orange aglow
Due to the dissipating light
Daytime soon turns into night.

The moon is shining way up high
With the twinkling stars in the sky
The sky is black, the moon is white
To help mariners navigate their way at night
But all too soon the stars disappear
We know a new day will soon be here.

Sometimes on a crystal morn
I wake up early to see the dawn
Shades of amber fill the sky
As the sun starts rising high
Then the clouds all fluffy and bright
Break the amber and blue with shards of white.

Ann-Marie Williamson

As Sunset Dims

As sunset dims and shadows fall
On silent waters, clear and calm
When daylight skies exchange attire
For evening dress in all its charm . . .
'Tis just another scene I see,
One of many I've espied
Within this vale so dear to me
Enthrals my soul with loving pride.

When morning comes to rearrange
The scenic blush of its new day,
Whate'er the weather should aspire
The vale will surely have its say . . .
And as the valley speaks to me
With echoed volume in its voice
My heart will thrive on every word
My soul will evermore rejoice.

Marian Theodora Maddison

Came The Day

I saw the host upon the hill
The joy of life to fulfil
The songbirds in chorus trill.

A blazon of colour to behold
Before one's eyes a cloth of gold
Oh, wondrous sight in the wold.

Came the day when a sight as this
To blink an eye, what joy you'd miss
To stare in wonder at nature, bliss.

To walk in England's pleasant land
Adventure unfolds like Alice in fairyland
In awe at such grandeur by God's almighty hand.

This scene is likened to some Passion play
Would that I kneel upon this cloth of gold to pray
That in my soul I'm blessed, came the day.

John Clarke

I Choose Nature As My Bride

I choose Nature as my bride
For in her I have found my pride.
Her over-much beauty be what makes me
Demand her Excellency as my wifey.

The nice-lookingness of the sky
And Mount Everest up high;
The glorious greenness of the plant
And the birds with their chant;

The natural songs of the seas
And the breeze and the bees;
The setting sun in the horizon
And the brilliance of the dawn's son.

Surely shall become my offspring
Always, especially during spring.
For I have given my love to Nature -
As the Mother of all my nurture.

Bolaji St Ramos

New Life

Springtime means new life!
Daffodils yellow! will open their petals to delight us.
We are aware of birds singing, and the trees bursting green.
Look and see the humble snowdrop, so fragile yet so perfect in itself.
And in the ponds life is there!
Children with nets, wonder what is to be found . . .
A worm? A frog? It does not matter!
All is created by God, the miracle of life begins again!
The mother ewe loves her lamb!
And God loves us too.
Do not be lonely or afraid,
God is only a prayer away.
God bless you.

Joan M Waller

A Bright Jewel

(Thoughts on a perfect autumnal day - November 15th 2007)

As I look around me on this autumn day,
The sky is cloudless; it is stretching endlessly
Away in alternating shades of sapphire . . .
Gazing hypnotically at the trees, a tricolour
Effect, strikes the eye; amber, and
Green and pomegranate; the whole aura
That surrounds the senses from ground
To sky . . . is summed up in one word -
Iridescent; shifting to tortoiseshell of
Cat, and white and black of magpie . . .
The exposed birds' nests within smoky
Brown boughs and emeraldine leaves; the sun
Dazzles; the core of life? . . . A bright jewel.

Valerie Hall

Nature's Power

A walk in the country down leafy lanes
View the fields full of swaying golden grain
Nature has provided this panoramic scene
When the sun shines down its warming beam
Lazy white clouds float in the blue sky
Birds are singing and flying up high
Hedgerows around the fields growing so strong
Containing the animals that eat all day long
The breeze making ripples over the ponds
Of walking in the country I am so very fond
Nature keeps on going and never sleeps
While she prepares for us so many treats
For her actions she never gives reason
Why or when she changes the season
She helps all things to flourish and grow
Using the sun, rain and the moonlight glow
The power of nature is wonderful and grand
Please God it never gets into the hands of Man.

LAG Butler

The Hard Outer Layer

The twitter and swoops of the sandmartins
Racing over the seaweed mats, smelling in the midday heat
Flies feeding on the salty weed
The high-flyers feeding on the flies
High above the tide-line the colony of birds pop in and out of
                                                    their sandy burrows
The cliff looking like a giant pepper pot
The black holes a welcoming rest after the glare of the sun
Thoughts of ice cream on the minds of the children
Parents discussing exorbitant prices for holiday accommodation
They appear not to see or hear the birds
They never lift their eyes to the beauty around them
The hard outer layer of living has not been penetrated yet
It needs just a chink to be breached for them to experience the simple
                                                    beauty of a shell, a pretty stone
Children do not even put their toes in the water
When I was little it was sandals off and a paddle
I can still remember my dad's bony toes embracing the cold North Sea
With my little chubby toes like little fat fish next to his.

H J Clark

Plant

Every thirsting flower will raise
To God on High a song of praise,
And by its glorious petals roam,
To seeing eyes from soil's home,
Where honeyed radiance in its cloy,
Brings frenzied bee, in sweet annoy,
And stamen's love sips kissing's heart,
Where rich delight proves pollen's dart,
Oh! ne'er could then such lovely be,
As the plant that moves freely.

Barry Bradshaigh

Walking With Trees

Looking for a cure from care?
Take a walk in the woods.
You will find it there -
whatever the season.
Snow, rain, hail or shine,
you don't need a reason.
Walk with the swaying trees,
they will ease your pain,
breezes rustle through the leaves
bringing soft rain.
Take a walk at night-time,
silent owls glide,
honeysuckle perfumes all,
small woodmice hide.
Try walking with trees,
Nature's cure for daily living,
creatures live as creatures should,
above the birds are singing.

Ivy Allpress

Gardens

Meanwhile I will wait,
It was scribbled on the chipped plank of a faded bench,
in a garden that looked deserted.
A moment passed and a bird dropped the greenish white excrement
in a fit of personal temper.
The barks of old trees became murals
and the huddled went ahead with their zooming conspiracies,
their human superiority and fetish exchanged,
love under the shades,
of a city garden is a sight,
like a free verse scattered everywhere,
but there are pockets of silence in these places,
where muffled mouths produce scandals
and live out the life.

Rizwan Akhtar

Observe And Ponder

Let's not forget
The sound of a lamb's bleat
Learning how to suck its mother's teat
The season that brings blossoming power
Whether an egg to life or bud to a flower
Its obedience to God's natural order
Climbing, bedding or border
Many a plant basking in beauty
Strawberries and tomatoes tasty and fruity
All a signal that the clock still turns
And all examples that a child learns
When studying what we're all taught
But do we appreciate it when flowers and meat are bought?
When a lamb goes to slaughter
Do we think it's a sheep's son or daughter?
Or when we pay for a bunch of flowers
That in its bed it no longer towers
I don't think that this natural cycle should stop
So let's not forget this array of wonder
Take time to observe and to ponder.

Stacey Morgan

Nature's Wonder

Driving through the countryside is really so amazing,
To see the cows busy grazing,
Young lambs skipping to and fro.

The fields filled with hay, wonderful on a summer's day.
We are lucky, you and I,
To see the wonders that nature gives.

The sun, the birds that fly, a cooling breeze,
The rustle through the trees.
A shady nook, a babbling brook.
The wonders of nature wherever we look.

Terri Brant

April Blossoming

With shades of earthly colour,
With beautiful wisteria growing,
With a fragrance so divine and magical,
As night-time moths dance underneath the moonlight.

Nature dazzles the eyes with wonder,
Where the song lark sings superbly,
During the morning dreamy walk,
A thousand gossamer threads shine like pure silver,

Whilst Madame walks pickin' wild fruit and flowers,
Where the sweetpea is king of all she surveys,
So surreal and ghostly is the morning forest,
Prolifically in abundance, with a million ladybirds flying,

As a chorus of songbirds fight and dance,
Like a jewel in the night a kingfisher flies,
Past shimmering water, where water nymphs dive and hide,
Spring, the life giver of the new year, and tide

Timeless and wedded to nature with yellow gorse,
Painted by the great artist's hand, are daffodils and poppies,
Carnations, tulips, lavender, bluebells amongst the bowers,
Cherry sunflowers, orchids and the blossoming rose,

Where a great queen has been walking through snowdrops,
Through the April blossoming where mistletoe is seen,
Enduring giant clematis budding through the sunlight,
Within the hidden garden plants are lush and bright,

Through the traditional landscape,
Is a spring breeze where daisies and buttercups grow,
With ferns and dandelions and the chestnut tree,
With oak and ash, elm and silver birch, lay underneath,

A wondrous carpet of bluebells as I spy Madame,
Reading her classical love poetry book.

James Stephen Cameron

Mother's Nature

Clean water splashing against the mountain rocky face
Transparent, bluey-jade ocean working hard
Sending its powerful waves forward and back again and again
A warm summer breeze gently glides
Over my body and face, through my brunette hair
For a few seconds, blows everywhere
The golden sandy beach is lovely and warm
Under my tiny feet, it goes between my toes
As I kneel down to pick up a few shells and stones -
Later I climb the rocky mountain
Nearly reaching the clear blue sky
One by one people have gone, leaving me alone, to enjoy
The breathtaking scenery, whilst inhaling unpolluted fresh air -
I sit on the grassy mountain top
Slurp a can of fizzy pop, dangle my tiny legs over the mountain edge
Alone but feeling safe
I look over the peaceful ocean, whilst looking at
The dramatic summer evening sky,
The odd JJ aircraft flying over very high catches my eyes
Whilst the odd puffy white cloud slowly floats by
Slowly the sun starts to drop, putting on a dramatic magical show
Terracottas, reds, orange, yellow, purple and rustic browns,
The sun, how like a massive ball of fire
As it slowly melts into the ocean and ground.
Now it's dark - Miss Sun swaps shifts with Mr Moon
As he switches on his light all the tiny diamond stars twinkle
extremely bright
Just enough for me to stand, ready to walk home
I say, 'Goodnight.'

Paulette Francesca Sedgwick

The Highlands

Looking north on to the bleak, lonely moors
Dark and silent as the night falls, and
Watching the golden eagle swoop down
From the sky, listening to the sighing of
The wind as it rustles through the trees
And hearing the sound of gurgling water
As the stream gushes noisily around some
Jagged rocks, descending several stony
Shelves down into a deep pool surrounded by
Birch trees, their twisted roots like
Tentacles thrust deeply into the soft black
Earth covered with a thick green moss
And seeing the phantom stag drinking its fill
Of the pure clear, life-giving waters, high up
In the snow-swept mountainous peaks, its
Silhouette standing proudly outlined against
A clear night sky.

G Morrison

A Dragonfly

A dragonfly rises, flying out across,
Civitatis orbis terrarum,
An atlas of European cities, hum,
Below the beauty and wonder, no loss
As its long legs below it, do toss:
Civitatis orbis terrarum,
I viewed in fear as it sat by rum,
Landing in my pub, by barmaid's boss:
She walked past it, to my great relief,
Her boots did not crush it: the insect,
Rose, flew up to the bar shelf, in mischief,
Again rested on glass, spirit to reflect:
The joy, wonder of European skies,
Raises its wings, outside it flies.

Edmund Saint George Mooney

Grey Sky In Summer

This day the sky is grey,
but look again and see
the mass of billowing dove-grey clouds.
The palest ones almost white.
Some like woodsmoke ash and
softest slate-grey.
Smaller ones like a string of pearls.
So serene the sky looks.
No wind blows to disturbs the clouds
or stirs the grasses in the meadow.
The hedgerows silently display their colours.
Berries ripening.
No movement.
A quietness like a cloak envelops the land.
The air is still
but with a gentle warmth.
Nature seems at rest this sunless morning.

Margaret Miles.

The Soul Of The Waters

Seals are above the scorching
Soul of the northern waters
The caribou has arrived
The sun is returning
Into the wilderness
The soul is migrating
The light is blinding
Seals are there calling from
The frozen soul of the waters
Dreams, guardian spirits
In the form of animals
The medicine men following
Following inner instructions . . .
The soul of the waters
Is forever changing . . .
With every day of the year.

Mariana Zavati Gardner

A Recipe For Spring

What a lot of entertainment
    From some old bread that has gone stale
Normally it would be just thrown away
    Yet, now it has created this tale.

A rewarding fine sight will emerge just for you
    And, all you need is some bread that is old
Eventually (it'll take just a minute or two)
    You will see colours so clear and so bold.

A slice, or two, of old bread - that is all
    Broken up into 'bite-size' pieces
Then just scatter them around your garden
    Across lawns, by paths and near niches.

Return to the comfort of your home
    Pull up a chair, and just wait
It won't take long - just you see
    Your patience will reward you - it's fate!

A brave one will appear by your unwanted bread
    Feasting quickly whilst abating its fear
Then the others of its kind soon arrive alongside
    For they all have the same idea!

With hungry mouths to feed at home
    There really is no time to waste
Just gobble some bread down quickly
    No time to savour the taste.

After stealing a second for their own meal
    They gather as much as they can
In their mouths, they cram it all in
    This banquet provided by Man.

It is spring, and the weather is sunny
    Refreshing - each morning, and clear
They race for some food for their families
    Before others of their type draw near.

Males and females taking turns
    From safe distances, one acts as the lookout
For the dangers that are always present
    Whilst out 'shopping' for food, there's no doubt.

Their children, back home, are all waiting
    Reliant on your old stale bread bits
The sparrows, blackbirds and finches
    Also magpies, jackdaws and tits.

So, your pieces of stale bread are not wasted
    When broken up and strewn all around
You'll be visited by all different birds each time
    When they spot you down there on the ground.

It is a true recipe for spring
    Pass it on, and let it be heard
When your unwanted food gets 'recycled'
    Filling the bellies of new baby birds.

Remember, all it takes is some bread,
    Good intentions and patience, 'tis true
Your reward is the trust from the parents
    When their babies they will bring to show you.

With fluffy feathers, and now as big as their parents
    Though certainly nowhere near as wise
The young fledglings all baying to be fed at once
    In your garden, right in front of your eyes.

A small token of kindness from you each day
    With no baking involved on your part
This simple recipe for spring has unfolded
    Warm images to keep in your heart.

Joanne Hale

Spring Will Be A Little Early This Year

Today thoughts are sprinkled with a spring,
A spring that is sprinkled with yet another thing,
A thing that is yellow and smells quite like grass,
A flower so simple, I'm longing to ask;

What do you do when winter does fall?
When darkness surrounds and frost freezes all?
Down in the burrows where roots take their hold,
Finding the pathways that never grow cold.

And when do you take the chance to step out?
Inching your way through the roof and the drought
Of sunshine and warmth, of light and of scent,
The earth so unfriendly, yet always you meant

That hello you put forwards,
The hello made from smiles,
And now you are blooming, yet still, all the while
Your roots will not last long,

Your bulb has stretched till
It's broken its mould and you are here still,
Inviting us all to open our eyes,
To feel this new warmth brought forth with blue skies.

But too early, I ask, too early you've come,
It's winter still here, but it's not winter sun,
You've answered a call, but I fear it's too soon,
The answer is desperate; your petals may swoon,

And fall to the roses that capture our hearts,
No bluebells, they're lonely,
The snowdrops depart,
And gaily we wander without any care,

You light up with yellow that reflects the spring air,
But soon, far too early, yet I love with despair,
Addicted to living just as you only can,
Stretching with such green flimsy care.

And breathing the sweetness, dispelling all fear,
Forgetting the notion that spring is now here,
Not caring of why or how we did meet,
Now drinking the nectar brought forth from its heat.

Joanna Wallfisch

A Storm Is Coming

The shuddering sky is heavy
Creaking and groaning
Under the weight of its
Tempestuous burden.

Craving release
Its fury pent up
Like a thousand celestial hounds
Baying for blood.

Rage
Boiling
Burning
Exploding

But its power and its passion
Are not destructive forces
They cleanse, invigorate, revive
The naked, pockmarked earth.

The thick, suffocating air becomes
Soft and fragrant
A serene sigh escapes from the liberated sky
Restful and at ease.

Life begins.

Joanne Starkie

Return Of Spring

Oh glorious, victorious spring,
Triumphant over cold adversity,
Bursts upon this earth once more,
With all its versatility.

Blossoms in profusion all around
Adorn the trees and meadows green,
Multi-colours to delight the eye,
Nature paints a colourful scene.

New life surrounds us every day,
A privilege to behold rebirth
Of all creatures great and small,
Their right to live upon this Earth.

Summer soon replaces spring,
Flora and fauna reign supreme,
Such wonders of nature to view with awe,
But to return to spring is my dream.

Although each season displays its beauty
The countryside has much in store,
From flowers, fruit and seeds of autumn
Spring is the one I adore.

Doreen Kowalska

Springtime

Spring is here again.
Lighter mornings and lighter evenings.
The sunshine high in the sky.
Daffodils, tulips and bluebells flowering.
Blossoms such a delight.

Summer clothes begin to appear,
Holidays now being booked.
Children play in park and garden,
The cricket season now begins.

People walk in hill and vale.
Picnics the order of the day.

The most beautiful sight
Here in the Dearne Valley,
Is the woodlands now returning,
Returning to grow again,
Where once were the mines.

The woodlands our forebears knew,
Now again in full leaf.

Thank God for spring.

Janet Cavill

Springtime

Springtime, and the cherry tree blossom
in the corner of the front garden
signifies that summer lies ahead;
and happy children sing and dance,
welcoming the spring as sunny as themselves.
Winter-born babes have so much
to look forward to
in the months that lie ahead;
much happier and sunnier
than the drab December days
which welcomed them into the world.
Nature's symphony of new leaves
rustling in the springtime breeze,
and songster birds with families to feed
must surpass in sweetness
the music of all time,
no matter how sweet Man has made it.
How thankful we must always be
for springtime, and the blossom
on the cherry tree.

Margaret Worsley

Frosty Night

One-forty in the early hours,
November the twenty-second,
I cannot sleep and so I write
On a bitterly cold and frosty night.
The time goes so slowly, the air so chill,
The moon is so bright and the dark so still.

One-fifty in the early hours
and so to bed I go and hope the darkness
finds me sleep, and takes away the chill.

Joan Kniveton

Urban Or Landscape

It does not matter, where you live
This time of year, has much to give
Choirs in trees, welcome each new day
Such golden treasures, are on display.

Newborn lambs, will leap and prance
In many fields, coupled flowers dance
From the sky, we see a rainbow's dome
We know once more, spring has come home.

Time to put forward, seasonal clocks
On urban streets, espy the odd wild fox
Hedgehogs and dormice, are very wary
The human being, can be very scary.

We know spring, is well and truly here
When Robin Redbreast, begins to appear
Lepidopterists come out, in their swarms
To see golden wings, as the weather warms.

Streams and rivers, continue to flow
Up in the air, blackbirds will crow
Spring spreads a blanket, far and wide
In the urban cities, and the countryside.

Like fresh blood, injected into the veins
We can spot the wildlife, in country lanes
The hours of each day, are extended
As winter's damage, is gradually mended.

Fields of yellow, will continue to thrive
Emotions run high, glad to be alive
Early mornings have, a nip in the air
Meadows no longer, look bleak and bare.

Waking to see the sun shining, each day filled, with a golden lining
Optimism is what it will bring, that wonderful season
we know as spring.

B W Ballard

Birth Of A Season

As the life begins to meditate,
To the intricate birth of the start.
What was sullen grey, now psychedelic,
All shades, tones, all colours.

The virginal start to the cycle begins,
And the flowers start to breathe.
The sounds, the smells of a new season,
Cometh, the beginning of life.

And while I watch the flowers grow,
All the wild babies are born.
Innocence of springing lambs,
Waiting for the summer sun.

I come alive amongst all this,
With the dull of winter gone.
Appearing safe from my womb,
Positive is lingering, the birth is here.

William Adam

Spring

In winter things look grey and bleak.
Spring heralds in the new life we seek
As the sun breaks on a new dawn
Birds welcome in the new morn
Daffodils raise their proud yellow heads
Colourful crocuses cover the flower bed
Spring has arrived in all its glory
Mirroring in nature the Easter story
What we thought was dead and gone
Raises up and still lives on.

S J Sanders

Ode To Pollen

The beech tree is blooming
and all through the house
this lady is sneezing
and being a grouch

Outside sun is shining
now springtime is here
I'm longing for winter
and I'm being fair

My garden rejoices
in colour and song
my sneezes rival
a blackbird sing-a-along

It's not that I don't like
the spring in the air
but I can't take the pollen
making my eyes tear.

Lila Joseph

Bluebells

I came upon the magic
One crisp springtime day
And it's true, such a beautiful sight
Has never gone away.
The green trees of the woodland
The bluebells that carpeted the ground
Filling the air with a fragrance
That wrapped me all around.
Now if life is at its darkest
And all seems sad it's true . . .
I remember that magic picture
And life starts to renew.

Joyce Hudspith

Morello Cherry Blossom

(My garden on Friday 10th May 1985, at 10.20am)

Morello cherry blossom, virgin-white against the sky,
I look up to you in wonder and I 'gasp a wondrous sigh'
At your bridal-bouquet beauty tipped by spears of pretty green,
And I bow - as if by duty - at the 'marvel' of the scene,
With the whitish sky going heavy as there's thunder in the air,
And the birds are homeward winging - a-rushing everywhere . . .

Now a yellow finch has flown in to land on my washing line,
And to look for darting insects that go buzzing all the time
In my 'green and yellow' garden with 'virgin-white' against the sky,
Where the lilac's almost blooming - 'pink' clusters by and by . . .

And beneath its pretty laden branches, where finished wild violets lay,
The bluebells 'are about to open' their faces to the day . . .

And the yellow forsythia petals that have fallen to the ground
Will soon be topped with white confetti once the storm has
blown it down . . .

And the daffodils a-dreary - each hang their tired heads;
Like the rest of springtime's bloomings, are mostly dried and dead . . .

But the rhubarb's in full glory - well-watered by some rain;
And - with puddings, pies and bottling - I've much from
that 'to gain' . . .

So, my Morello cherry blossom, virgin-white before the fall,
Standing there like some goddess with arms stretched out to all,
I look up to you 'in wonder' at *your moment* as you reign
Above my little garden in *your own royal domain* . . .

And, at last, when summer's over and your laden branches thick
With fruits as dark as damsons - then, your swollen gems I'll pick . . .

Mary Pauline Winter (nee Coleman)

Sprouted Spring This Season

This spring as life bounces back
I shall celebrate like never before

I shall send gifts to all
To the blind, a song lyrical of rainbow-coloured flowers
                                                sprinkled on leaves
To the deaf, a poem tuned on melody of cuckoo
To those who have lost sense of smell, words translating the fragrance
                                                of flowers

To the mentally challenged, a bouquet of innocent buds
To the paralysed, an inspiring tale of fresh leaf who rose from
                                struggling summer, depressing winter

To desert dwellers, a painting vibrant of spring hues
To friends, a collage of moments reliving our lifesprings
To lovers, a season scented nostalgic silent letter
To me, a prayer for life

This spring as life bounces back
I shall celebrate
This spring could mean a lot to many
But it means the most to me
As this one is my last
If the last one wasn't last already

To you I gift a warning note
Make the most of this spring
For the Earth is dying of a fatal fever too
So even for you this season is last of its kind
For next spring will be a few degrees warmer
For next spring could become a summer.

Soma Das

Sunshine And Showers

Sunshine and showers, flowers and trees
birds in the garden, the humming of bees.
Children out playing, laughing with joy
flying a kite, cuddling a toy . . .

Watching a baby asleep in its pram,
a teenager's smile, blackcurrant jam.
Seeing the postman bringing some mail,
Man's best friend wagging its tail . . .

Walking and fishing, paddling ashore,
eating fresh cockles, ice cream galore.
Colourful butterflies, wind blowing chimes,
writing a letter and poetic rhymes . . .

Soaking tired feet, such utter bliss,
someone to give you a butterfly kiss.
Having a hairdo that doesn't go wrong,
wearing new shoes that don't squeak a song . . .

Cooking a sponge with no sink in the middle,
making Welsh scones on Grandma's old griddle.
A game won at last by a favourite team,
Wimbledon tennis; strawberries and cream . . .

Sunshine and showers heralding spring
a time to smile and heartily sing . . .

M L Damsell

Remembering

So many things are written
About the joys of spring,
Of all the trees that blossom
And the many birds that sing.
But what about the other side
Of this familiar notion,
About the many other lands
On the far side of the ocean?

Some are dry and arid
Where it hardly ever rains,
And some are just the other way
With vast and flooded plains.
Many people in the world
Don't have enough to eat,
For others, just clean water
Is a very welcome treat.

How fortunate we are
In this green and fertile land,
For all our basic needs
Are found quite close to hand.
Remembering those in ravaged lands
We should thank our Lord on high,
For there, but for the Grace of God,
Go both you and I.

Doreen Williams

Lent

Living water hue - bayou-blue, mossy green -
In mid-March Lenten light now at dusk comes again,
Like living light dusk a wet March I once knew
When my heart beat so fast, so wild in its joy,
Wake, impatient for dawn - when I was a boy.

Damp winter-warm, morning-cool, calming breeze,
Still chill like love's thrill, freely groped as it pleased
Boldly in and about each little harbinger with ease,
Each soft-leaf, wild flower - gold, purple, white,
Who spanned every field, a host teeming and bright,
Who heralded wild violets could be deemed to appear
Beneath eaves of porches, beside doorstep and stair,
Near shadowed banks of sheer spring-rippled streams.

O, I hunted them there, rare treasures, where
Dark earth often dank, still smelled painfully sweet,
Where black soil wet-pressed my knees as I knelt
While wild violet, soft foliage brush-kissed my hands
As I felt for the place where the bud would arise
And blind-searched for the violet to behold in my eyes -
Mystic hue, power-red with cool wisdom of blue -
A tint more than colour, climbing higher than skies.

How each humble shy violet I gathered elated in pride
To be worn, urned or candied, to be taken inside
Home and heart, blood and sweet, in union of life
Consumed as a host - hope of glory, wisdom, love;
Yet, violets, as violet, diffused sorrow of doves.

Recalling wild violets this Ash Wednesday close
While blue light turns violet as night welcomes rain,
Into April once more I'll scout Lent's violet stain
To his lily's white sweet and red blood of his rose.

Edgar Wyatt Stephens

Spring

Longer daylight hours bring forth fresh, bright flowers.
Birds flit to and fro, always on the go:
Fighting and pairing, nesting and sharing,
Singing and mating, then watching and waiting
For eggs laid to hatch.
There follows the caring, continuous, wearing,
To feed young, and protect from the predator's snatch.

All nature seems moving: plants pushing and shoving
Their way through the earth;
Leaves unfurling, buds uncurling,
Lambs and fox cubs being born;
Fresh green shoots of grass and corn,
Silent growth, activity, everywhere in spring I see;
But what has it to do with me?

My own springtime is past, and I can feel aghast
At the decline of summertime!
I am no longer in my prime,
And autumn tints already show in hair and features.
Now the glow of winter fireside beckons more
Than going outside to explore,
And to experience everything
Which once awakened me to spring!

I feel I should spring into action! Satisfaction,
Energy, invigoration,
Seldom come from contemplation.
Yet, in all life there must be periods of torpidity,
Suspended animation, dearth,
Death and decay, to precede birth
And all the wonders it can bring
As hidden life breaks forth in spring!

Nancy Solly

A Place Called Vrnwy

Breezes flow gently over a calm lake leaving a fine weave of serenity
With a tower standing high over the water leaving an immense shadow
Lying across the brow a resplendent bridge enticing samples
                                                    of tranquillity
Water cascading from the depths winding itself to the river below

Scenes emerge as the majestic beauty awakes to life in the early morn
Dewdrops still glisten as birds drink from the nectar of the day
The rustle of leaves reminds you as the breeze breaks a calmer storm
Letting you know you are in a place that could be far away

Wildlife hides in hedgerows escaping the midday sun on high
That breathes away humidity until the evening arrives late
Tall trees stand waiting to cast long shadows beneath a clear sky
A sight known only to those who tarry by the shores of slate

There are stories of life before when a valley stood proud and green
When people walked the land below while children played their games
Lying beneath the coolness of the day as shadows dance
                                                    to make a dream
With peace as you sit and daydream of a village that keeps its name

Though man-made forms secured its fate, given all the beauty
                                                    there is no gate
A covered peaceful valley using mountains as a shield to cover
                                                    all its charm
A strong and fulfilled village lies deep inside hidden in its fate
A pretty place called Vrnwy found standing quiet and calm.

J Barker

Autumn Month

Now the trees stand tall but bare
Away from the summer months we did share
Gone is the beauty, that once was here
When birds sang with praise and cheer

Now the leaves have fallen upon the ground
When once beauty was seen all around
We see the bracken turn from green to yellow
When once the twittering warble notes of the swallow

Were heard. Usually produced on his wing
But, now we may hear the robin, sing
A characteristic general cockiness from this fellow
But, when it rains, he shelters in the meadow

Through the hollow of the trees, still standing bold
Away from the boisterous winds, out of the cold
When in summer, the fields were filled with flowers
As the sun shone around, bringing the shining hours

Now that autumn months, brings the skies grey
Perhaps, yet again, we may see a sunny day
Sweeping the swarmy mist away, through the morn
Then clearly is seen the friendly robin, at dawn

Showing his red breast, with his mate, on the bare trees
Distinctively seen, and made through God's nature so free
Who made the seasons, summer, autumn, winter and spring
Which, may touch our hearts, listening to blackbirds sing.

Jean McGovern

Springtime

This is the month of the Maypole
And all the plants have new shoots.
When we put away the fire coal
And we put aside our boots.
We pass a cloud when May is out
For summer is on its way.
I can see the flies are about
For they too think they can stay.

For in this merry month of May
The farmers set out to work.
This is the time they boost their hay,
They can't afford to shirk.
For years ago they had Maypole time
And they always had great fun.
So now today it's not so fine
But where now is everyone?

Margaret Burtenshaw-Haines

Just Round The Corner

The twelfth of March was a bitter cold day
With a searing breeze and skies of grey
Yet a thrush and a chaffinch managed to sing
And a pair of carrion crows on the wing
Performed a courtship display.

In the lea of a bank, celandines were showing
And the young leaves of nettles had begun growing
While in the feathery branches of a lofty beech
Far out of every predator's reach
Noisy rooks at their nests were toing and froing.

Snow from the dykebacks was fast disappearing
As a pair of hares frolicked in the clearing
A wren found his voice and started to sing
Surely this was the start of spring
From what I was seeing and hearing.

E D Bowen

On A Storm

Hark! Hark! Thunder hails its own arrival,
Like the approach of a marching army,
Heard but unseen, only heavy clouds and heavy brows
Betray its arrival; the very air throbs
As witness to its awesome presence.
In one fearful crack, mounted tension:
Shattered. Like a mirror breaking above a bed
Heavy shards of rain descend in anger,
Beating where it falls, intent and purposive.
The air smells of a Concordia Discors
As bruised earth and foliage
Are snapped, as if phials of smelling salts,
Reviving the fresh odour that heralded their arrival.
An armed host of looming, clamourous clouds
Hammer out chorus after chorus of pointed darts,
Piercing delicate beds and canopies of foliage,
Spurning the parched soil; desperate only to drink,
To find its thirst being quenched
By some vengeful, intolerable father.
Its fit of apoplectic rage expires soon enough,
Anger is diffused, dark clouds recede,
And despite this terrible patriarchal interposition
Earth and plant alike are grateful for their gift.
No wounds or scar tissue blemish the scene
For this terrible explosive only creates,
Adds, does not subtract:
The air is fresh once more,
Breeze now only ripples upon skin, upon leaves.

Stephen Tuffnell

April In Lincolnshire

Spring speaks softly
in this county.
Disturbing winter's menace,
the sun guides icebergs
from its skies.

A motion in the days
teases wolds to life.
Beside margins buds
grow fat
and blackbirds court.

In a wash of lemon light,
farms shake off their trance.
Warmth unwinds the air,
installs itself in earth,
and eases rheumatic bones.

Children strip winter
speech and catch ladybeetles.
Grandparents imagine
a world of ancient hope
in Eden-green.

Hawthorn breathes
through veils of rain.
Gulls on saltmarshes
shriek as membranes
crack.

Churchyards are buttered thick
with Lenten lilies,
Everywhere love's fever
begins shrill
Hallelujahs.

Lincoln shivers.
Waits for its tourists
to recapture Lindrum Hill -
and bring a cure
for silence.

Derek Webster

Orchid

My beautiful red-lunged orchid,
Very soon will die;
So pure and delicately poised,
As a swan, its wings held high . . .
With careful shoots of pollen gems,
Their feather bedding splayed;
Upright against the grey surround,
As a warrior blindfolded,
Unafraid.

My beautiful red-lunged orchid,
It's always almost time to go:
So fragile and courageous,
But these are things I know . . .
Tall, graceful and untainted -
As an angel set to soar
Over laughing children's gardens,
- Not built to live in war.

My beautiful red-lunged orchid,
I'm glad we spent this time;
It's right that you'll be leaving soon,
Too innocent for a life like mine . . .

My beautiful red-lunged orchid,
Not mine, but God's: I'll cry;
In grief of the time I'll remember when
Perfection was meant to die.

Denise Delaney

The First Spring

It was spring when the council moved us there,
'We shall have a new house,' my mother said
'There'll be trees and fields and clean fresh air.
You will have your own room - and your own bed.
Our house is number two hundred and four,
There are two pretty girls who live next door.'

One was called Lizzie and the other one Jo
Who thrilled me with tales of Camelot.
They showed me flowers that I did not know.
Bluebell, primrose and bright forget-me-not.
We played in their secret den by the stream
Where we made daisy chains fit for a queen.

We caught silken butterflies in bare hands
Then set them free while we chased another.
We fought many battles in foreign lands
And crept through the long grass under cover.
Lizzie held me tight and taught me to kiss,
I knew there would never be another spring
                                        like this.

John Eccles

Unfaithful Friends

All through the winter
You gather round my table,
Elegant males in robes of sable,
Or vests of red or brown and white.
Dainty ladies, with dark eyes bright.
You're plump and round, I watch with awe
The depletion of my own food store.
Suddenly you're gone, no sign of thanks.

Noisy singing awakens me at daybreak
As love floats high heralding the spring,
Twisting and turning on outspread wing.
Urgent now to win their lady's favour,
Build a shelter, and reap the fruits of labour.
Expectant fathers strut and preen
For expectant mothers lapped in green.
I sit in the tree shadows watching.

When winter gales take the place of leaves
You'll bring your hatchlings here to feed,
At my bird table.

Margaret Wilson

Spring Is Here

I open wide my window
Birdsong fills the air
Gaze in wonder at the sky
A sky gleaming gold and blue
Gone is the winter.
The corn is ripening
The stream runs clear
Shine on showers
Spring is here.

Fragrant fruit and fragrant flowers
Beds are full of colour
Pansy, poppy and hyacinth-blue
In a breeze as soft as thistledown
Lilies that dance just for you
Hawthorn blossom flushed in rosy light
Heady perfume just to give delight.

On the wooded hill
Tender tips of green light up the trees
Bluebells look cool in the shade
Drops of drew cling to their blades
Hang with bloom the snowy bough
The cherry by the woodland path
Tell us spring is here at last.

Beth Izatt Anderson

The Escape Of Spring

Spring, still enchained by Winter's hold,
Sought eagerly to break away
From all his bitter, numbing cold.

From white of snow to white and gold
Of snowdrops, aconites and may;
Yet, still enchained by Winter's hold,

With grief and tears begged to unfold
Her gentle treasures to the day;
But, still enchained by Winter's hold,

Fair daffodils and tulips bold
Fritillarias with gentle sway
Were still enchained by Winter's hold.

Treacherous snow he sent, to enfold
And stifle every quickening ray
Still to enchain by his cruel hold

Sweet spring, but she unrolled
Her treasures in their rich array;
She defied him, loosed his hold
And broke his chains of numbing cold.

Margaret Ballard

In The Bosom Of Creation

I loved my mountain home
where rugged remnants
of an ancient volcano
soared starkly to the heavens,
like gigantic pillars
supporting the
starry canopy
of the firmament.

I have marvelled;
lingering on a darkened hillside;
at the starry multitude above;
the spiritual significance of the heavens;
the beauty of that symbol of our lives' direction -
the Southern Cross.

I have reflected in humility
the beneficence of the Great Creator,
I breathed in wonder,
'Lord, how great Thou art.'

Patrick L Glasson

A Field Into Harvest

A field white
into harvest
where seeds blow
everywhere.
A field
north-east, south-west
so full, to be blessed.
A time of harvest
that appears
of poppies to see.
Wilderness of poppies
nurtured in time to be
ripe into harvest.
Seeds begin to stir -
and fully grow.
Steadfast, lives flow.
Poppies that are nurtured
grow splendid and tall.
Seeds then fall.

Maureen Thornton

Take A Walk On The Wild Side

North Devon's as good as it gets
If you live in a cage or are hand-fed as pets
Outside it's chemicals, hedgecutter and cars
Wild bird survival would be better on Mars

It's no lark having flown here to breed
Open field nice and green, just what I need
Laid a nice healthy clutch, everything's looking OK
Trundle, trundle, crush, crush, spray, spray.

What's the margin for? Watch the pheasant she's more clever
Hedgerow edge nice and dry from the weather
Out they all popped and chasing Mum down the road
Squashed the lot of them with his Michelins, the fat toad

How about me then? I'm your average Reynard
It's that horn again and they're pressing me hard
Beneath the noise and din I feel fangs sinking in
But why do they smear my blood on her chin?

Fancy your chances at being a Brock?
TB has put the badger in their dock
Traps; gas or dogs which is worse?
Drink your milk. Dairy farming has brought them this curse

Listen you lot, there's no doubt
You wouldn't want my life, your humble brown trout
Try gulping down some dirty green slurry
I guarantee you don't wake up in a hurry

How about me then? Two thousand miles I've just flown
Just can't help doing it, it's my need to reach home
But where's my barn? Why is that house in my hollow?
I feel so choked up it's difficult to swallow

Nobody has more hedgerows then North Devon, that's a fact
If only they're managed by the countryside act
But by munching up nests and disturbing our rest
It's you lot! You humans that we think are pests.

Charles Keeble

It's Nature

Bob Robin has perched in a nearby tree
And is chirpily singing away
He 'puffs' out his red breast for all to see
And he'll sing on and off all the day.

The thrush and the blackbird hopping around
Are joined by a cheeky young sparrow
They hunt for some worms or grubs in the ground
Or the rubbish heaped up in the 'barrow'.

Starlings are circling high over the house
And the dove to his mate gently coos
The owl hovers quietly in search of a mouse
But - the sparrowhawk is out on the cruise.

Putting some birdseed out on the lawn
The pigeons are first to arrive
They swoop in vast numbers and plunder the corn
Like honeybees swarming a hive.

Butterflies busy around in the flowers
While blue tits peck wildly at nuts
Squawking old crows leave their high leafy bowers
And the jackdaw around proudly struts.

Under the pile of old rotting logs
For woodlice their favoured abode
While out in the garden hop tiny green frogs
And maybe an ugly old toad.

It's evening and out comes a prickly hedgehog
Which sniffs around an old box
In shadows, a movement, it could be a dog
But no, it's a wily old fox.

Whatever the weather, come sunshine or rain
In summer or long winter's strife
These creatures will visit the garden again,
It's nature, in essence, it's life.

D J Wooding

Sonnets For Late Spring

Upon a hillock strewn with golden flowers
I stood, a lonely pilgrim in delight
With Mother Nature in her glorious might;
And as the rising sun chased spring's late showers
Far beyond the seas, those hidden powers
Of wind, of sky and earth, of day and night
Wrought new wonders chaste to sound and sight
Arising as from cool and shaded bowers.
For from a verdant meadow just below
The knoll, a crystal stream of ceaseless song
Now heralded the sunrise, bidding dark
And gloom retire; and soon, with motion's flow,
His spiral flight rose up from nestlings' throng -
New morning's royal harbinger, the lark.

I strolled through verdant meadows rich with gold
As ox-eyed daisies vied with cowslips sweet
And tender; and beneath my velvet feet
A thousand buttercups stood up young and bold,
Shaking off the early morning cold.
I raised my eyes to distant fields of wheat
And corn, then strained my ears to hear the bleat
Of far-off sheep within some wandering fold;
And somehow knew that I was on a quest
For truth, but what that truth was I knew not -
I only knew that something drew me on:
Just as a host invites an honoured guest,
Truth beckoned me towards my chosen lot;
And I had precious thoughts to feed upon.

Robert D Hayward

Mother Nature

Mother Nature . . . Oh! Blue water. Oh! Soft globe . . .
I'm your slave; I'm your probe,
I'm for you . . . and for what you hold,
I'm a nature addict, this what I was told,
I like your fresh air . . . I like your breeze,
I like your flowery plants,
I like your shading trees,
I like all your little creatures . . .
Squirrels, wild rabbits, birds and trees,
I like the odours of your virgin prairies and farms,
I like the magical beauty of your countryside that charms,
Hunters, adventurers and lovers more . . .
Vagabonds and even fugitives who come for,
Seeking shelters to escape and hide,
Horse lovers and jockeys who ride,
I like your singing rivers that show and lean,
I like your floating swans going in twin(s),
I like the tiny alleyways that lead and mean,
Paths, short cuts, mews . . . all in green,
I like your braying donkeys and the barking dog,
I like the whistling winds and your splashy bog,
I like your orphan turtles and the leaping frog,
I like your frosty mornings and your ghostly fog,
I like your stylish gardens . . . I like your vogue,
I like everything in your Mother Nature,
But I don't deserve you . . .
Since I'm destroying you,
And myself . . . I'm a rogue!
I fear to miss the next spring,
When it comes barren, or may be frozen log!

Abder R Derradji

Spring

The change of season born from Earth's incline
The spring of life's renewal all can find
From colder days the sky becomes unveiled
In motion shown are whiter shades of pale

The Earth will follow suit and compass blend
Rebirth and budded life about to send
Of death from past existence life conceives
Where all is born and carried soft in breeze

And as I walk along this path reborn
Where bordered sides of vegetation worn
From left to right or front to back are seen
Colours just withheld in buds a-green.

This is a time of new and promise true
Where all of land and sky are held anew
To Earth a season seconds seem to Man
For in her instant is revealed her beauty charms.

Colin T C Mercer

Spring In Your Step

Say goodbye to languid winter
Open up your skies
Say goodbye to cinnamoned streets
Peer into the lemon lake
Spring-cool as tree-stained avenues
Greet the greenery and meet
The flowery finery
Of spring's glowing hello
With a wide heart to welcome
Summer's warm healing hands
Closing in on the cold
Stabbing mood of winter's frosty
No one, no how, nowhere bleakness
Say goodbye to the grey-brown blackness
Walk towards the tall, graceful eloquence
Of spring inspiring a talk in your step
And dropping love like an April shower
Laughing into your lap.

Julie Ashpool

A Lovely Garden

We look at the lawn, all square and neat,
Then look at the flowers whose perfumes are sweet.
The hanging baskets with begonias all aglow,
Their beautiful flowers trailing down below.
A rose arch that holds grapevines instead,
With grapes hanging down, it's the frost that they dread.
The ornaments there for all to see,
An angel, a tortoise, a rabbit by the tree.
The centre, a bird bath for the birds, it's quite tall.
Three children climbing it, one looks as if he might fall.
Two lovely lily ponds, full with goldfish,
Two banana trees, looking very swish.
An abundance of roses, all shapes and all sizes,
It's a pity their perfume won't win any prizes.
There are hollyhocks, geraniums and marigolds too,
With nasturtiums, fuchsias, snapdragons and lilies, to name just a few.
The bees buzzing gently, doing their work,
Dragonflies dipping and skimming over the pools,
                                    their duties they won't shirk.
The dogs lying on the lawn, at peace with the world,
And me sitting on a chair, with my feet underneath me and curled.

Zoe French

Changing Seasons

Springtime there across the way
winter winds blow in then the shaking of the leaves begin,
how wonderful the seasons change
and make a new display, making all the whiteness
across the hills and ways
almost lost from view
where once green grass and flowers grew.
Little footprints everywhere
through the woods and all around
a book of snow reads on the ground.
All winter through the flowers hide
beneath the frost and snow
until the warmth of springtime
tells them when to grow
then from the earth a race begins
to reach the springtime sun
and bring to life each sleeping flower
to bloom once more amid the woodland hills and vales
lovely green trees once more prevails

V N King

The Colt

It all began one spring day
In the quietness of the morn
A mare gave birth while in the field
And a lovely colt was born
Time went past and he grew up
Soon to run his race
At two he had outgrown himself
And couldn't keep the pace
His trainer had great faith in him
Each time he ran he knew
The great potential in his horse
Such speed was found in few
All too soon the big day came
And money placed on him
With jockey seated on his steed
The race would soon begin
With starters orders they were off
He jumped out of the gate
He kept tucked in beside the rails
To make sure he wasn't late
To break straight through and go for it
The winning post in sight
The colt had won the biggest race
And retired to stud that night.

Catherine Armstrong

Red Grass

In winter thereabouts the grass is red
And trees, their summer raiment shed,
Stand in pools of their own gold;
While russet bracken long since dead
Lies along the mountain's fold

Green colours only where the spruce,
Awaiting harvest and another use,
Stands planted neatly in its forest square.
A contrast to the randomness
Of nature, everywhere.

Then endlessly it seems, the rain
Tap, tap, taps upon the pane.
The days are short, and long the night,
But in the hearth the fire is bright
And now is time to play and sing
Content that after winter . . . spring.

Note:
The long rough hill grass dies in the winter
and in a sunny autumn, in particular
the long grass turns quite red.
Later as winter progresses the redness
goes and it turns light brown.

Richard Stead

Awakening

Parchment yellow, crinkled green
A patch of primroses to be seen,
Elfin-hooded snowdrops dance
Stately daffodils nod and prance.
Trees appear themselves to preen
Shivering branches sprouting green,
From a shaded nook beneath the trees
Bluebell perfume wafts in the breeze,
Cherry blossom; a mass of white
Chestnut candles give delight,
Hawthorn hedges pink and white amidst green
Wide-eyed daisies on lawn now are seen,
Yellow-billed blackbirds trill in morning light
Nesting sparrows squabble and fight,
Yawning, stretching, spring announcing
The dawning, of another awakening.

A Quinn

On Golden Pond

As the day begins to emerge,
Sparkling droplets of morning dew surround
The gold wings of insects flying busily around.
A hidden pond is masked by giant reeds.
Fractions of light begin to bounce off the silted water,
Highlighting a single lily pad.
A frog begins to sing a repeating song,
A dragonfly does a merry dance.
Slowly the sounds merge into a drifting reality,
For this is a place where one might wish
A dream to come true.
As if by magic a flow of life
Erupts upon creation each day
And a beacon is lit upon
The world.

R H Sunshine

Wonderful Nature

Snowdrops herald the onset of spring.
Such a wonderful sight,
As a new season begins.
Crocuses, daffodils; their colours supreme.
Nature is truly a most amazing thing.

The frost and snow are over yet again,
One can hardly credit that bulbs
Have bloomed again.
Garden birds are building their nests.
Such a labour of love
As they give it their best.

Longer, lighter evenings.
Time to tend to gardens again.
A walk with the dog,
A stroll in the park,
Then early tomorrow
I'll be up with the lark.

Joan Igesund

The Tree

Good to notice the tree,
Leaves dancing with joy and
Glowing in the calm summer light.
Breeze softly strokes my face,
A chance just to look,
Sense oneness of all life
Here in this present moment.

Even within chaos one can find
Stillness and clear seeing.
The mind may flutter yet, like
The leaves, can come back to
Quietness and calm,
Moments alone and with creation
Can gently calm all noise in oneself.

George Coombs

Sudden Spring

Spring - still not yet the kiss of spring!
Night now and day in equipoise,
But still the bluff north-easters bring
To last March days but little joys;
Reluctant buds still hide their head
And the bare hedgerows sleep abed.

The eager daffodils, that soon
Gold glory blaze for David's day,
By frost-tipped night, cool afternoon,
Sweet smiling, still prolong their stay,
And hearts uplift; nor have they ceased
Till they have hailed the Easter feast.

Then comes the long-expected breath
That lights upon the south-west shore,
And verdant life that lay beneath
In leaf and blossom breaks once more,
And Gwym and Gwen with hope begin
The day impatient spring bursts in.

Barrie Williams

Moonstruck

Did you see the moon last night?
Watch her make her wondrous flight,
Spinning beams of silvered light,
Flirting with the stars.

Did you watch her from below?
Her movement steady,
Determined, slow.
Clouds chased across her face
In aimless drift.

Along the Milky Way so vast
She sails, a ship without a mast,
Across an ocean dark and deep
Bedecked by stars which never sleep.

Dreams they spun
A million years ago,
Before their birth
To light the Earth,
Below.

Ann Wardlaw

Cherry Blossom

The cherry blossom
was like confetti in the air
the day that we met,
but I didn't love you then,
you were just a friend.

Love grew between us
like spring flowers
bursting into bloom,
and I loved you then,
more than just a friend.

Love grew stronger,
like saplings turn to trees
and the cherry blossom
was like confetti in the air,
the day that we wed.

Gillian Jones

Waltz Of The Willows

Flicker of moon on still waters
Reflection of crowds drifting by
Waltz of the weeping willows
Enthronged by laughter and chatter
I stand alone as the world drifts by

I can waltz with reflection on still waters
Weep with the willows that weep
Sing a refrain as stately reeds wave
To the lilies in harmony

A solemn performance
Gracefully conducted
The reeds and lilies
Praising the Lord
In the evening stillness.

Frances Gibson

Autumn

Gold and blue leaves hang serene,
Light paints a pretty autumn scene,
Clouds bear witness to the rain,
Autumn's dream comes once again,
Mellow apples grace the trees,
Where you and I once hurt our knees,
Football strikes the telly once more,
Close the windows, shut the door,
For an avalanche of change is here,
As moths, spiders and bats haunt the passing year,
In the hedges sparrows sing,
Welcome to the autumn king,
If you've been good you'll reap the fruits,
Like a riverside tree taking roots,
Don't miss the passing of the year,
All the wonders of nature are here.

N Evans

Love And Nature

Spring is a lovely time of year
The first of everything
The dainty snowdrops lead the way
Followed by the crocus and the daffodil
The hyacinths, tulips and wallflowers
Show forth their glowing colours
The trees burst out their buds and leaves
After thriving the winter bare
The birds start singing and build their nests
Soon their young will appear
The lambs and foals and calves leap forth
There is new life everywhere
It cheers you up to see all this
After long and dismal days
So let's enjoy the beauty that nature bestows
It does not cost a dime.

Eileen Finlinson

The Changing Seasons

What joy seasons bring, they fill your heart, make you want to sing
Spring daffodils, tulip buds peeping through, carpets of
$$\text{bluebells pink and blue}$$
Birds twittering waking anew, sounds of the cuckoo, owl and lark
Early morning dawn chorus singing in the dark

Buds on the hedges, buds on the trees, catkins dancing in the breeze
Prolific colour everywhere, summer's here - sun-drenched hair
Babbling brooks, walking boots, traverse over land
Take a walk along a beach, gather pebbles on the sand.

The nip in the air in the morning, means autumn is on its way
The changing colour of the trees, shimmering in the late
$$\text{afternoon breeze}$$
Walk through a wood, crunch leaves underfoot
Find windfall conkers - the old horse chestnut

Frosty nights come calling, winter approaches without delay
Wind, sleet, snow on the bough - trudging, trudging along somehow
Log fires burning, warm and cosy, stoke the fire - cheeks all rosy
See the moon all clear and bright, it seems to say, will be a frosty night

Let's count our blessings day by day, see all along the way
They are yours to enjoy, yours to explore -
God couldn't have given us anything more.

Marilyn Hine

Lingering

Were you there when the cowslips first appeared?
Or when the storm-cock sang to mark the falling rain?
Were you there when the scent of bluebell lakes
Drifted with the breeze along a country lane?

Were you there when the gentle pinks and golds
Of springtime brought its colour to the woods?
Were you there when young green leaves decked the trees
And the sun gave dapple-shade to warm the buds?

Or were you making money in the town
To buy yourself another this or that?
Or were you watching telly all the time;
Or listening to your Walkman in your flat?

We all must work to earn our daily bread -
But make a pause to watch the rainbow glowing bright;
We need the food and drink for sustenance -
But gaze awhile and see the owl in silent flight;

We need the clothes and the household stuff we buy -
But linger as you smell the flowers opening;
The TV and the Walkman have their place -
But leave them awhile and go and hear the blackbird sing.

Pauletta Edwards

A Song Frozen In Time

Frosty fingers spread and splay, to define
the hanging cobwebs shining like white gold
on bare branches, in the brittle sunshine.
Leaves are shed like fallen bodies of cold,
dead soldiers on battlefields of old.
But the hope-filled robin preens its scarlet breast,
perched on the stricken limbs still offering rest.

Sluggish green waters creep slowly along,
down the chilled ravine, passing staring trees.
While the wind throws back the hollow birdsong
on a swirling cyclone seeking to freeze
their small breaths, till feathered life, unhappily, flees.
Though winter jasmine beckons, with yellowed hand,
to the robin, perched, surveying the land.

Brown leaves of death float on the winterborne,
beside meadows stripped of wintergreens,
echoing the slowing heartbeat of forlorn
creatures, searching frozen soil for the means
to survive, yet still the robin preens.
While lacy white treachery fills the grey skies,
dispersing a blanket to cover its lies.

Footprints disappear in the drifting snow,
merging into nothingness in a world of white.
Houses shiver in blizzards sent to blow.
Relentlessly they snarl and growl and bite
at any living thing that comes in sight.
And now, the robin lifts its head and sings
against the fury of winter's sharpest stings.

Leafless alien figures stand in the dark,
surrounded by a landscape of empty space
where calm has descended, bringing a stark
reminder of how winter can displace
the labours other seasons all embrace.
But earth must take a rest through hibernation.
So robin folds his wings, in imitation.

Margaret Webster

The Beauty Of Our Earth

Down by the river the kingfishers fly
Down by the river the heron stands by
And the fish leap up - silver in the sun
There a man can find peace when day is done.

Trees cast their shade like a green parasol,
A haven of rest after life's busy toll,
This place that I know is not hard to find
Where the rippling brook soothes the tired mind.

Lie on the riverbank, under the trees
Where nothing is stirring, only the breeze,
Listen to the skylark joyfully sing
As upward he flies on fluttering wing.

Walk for a while by the cool riverside
Watch for the shy little creatures that hide
Out in the rushes or under the banks
And for all this beauty give God your thanks.

For it is God, with His love and care
Who gave this Earth for us all to share
The animals and birds know its true worth
It gives them food and shelter right from birth.

Responsibility we all must take
And for the future generations' sake
Respect this lovely Earth - it's not just ours
But to preserve it is within our powers.

Enjoy this beauty - it's a sacred trust
For those who will come after - it's a must
That we protect it with our caring
And leave them a world that's fit for sharing.

D N Wright

Nature's Beauty

Silver dew, sparkles on the gossamer web
First flickering light, shows above horizons,
The day begins with his rhythmic heartbeat
Bright yellow beaks call from nests on the greisens.

Smokey shimmers penetrate the hideaway
He moves to stand, lifting majestic head,
Across the dark, leaf-moulded forest floor
She hears his rumbling call, knowing his heavy tread.

The struggle finally ends, her body shudders
Their firstborn takes new breath, as Mother washes
His downy nose and soft, sweet mouth
Huge brown eyes gaze at multitudinous flashes

Trembling legs push the earth, he stands
On unsteady cloven hooves of purest white,
The glow of gold warms him as he gambols
Then walks proudly, as a young stag should . . .
Born of the purest love and light.

S Meredith

Sossusvlei

The day dawns brightly
As Nature serene
Wakes up in all her glory
For all her beauty to be seen.

The dunes all covered in an ethereal glow
The animals awaken and on their journeys go
Then the wind whips up the fine desert sand
Its fury so hard, one can hardly stand.

Suddenly the storm dies down
And every dune dons its evening gown
The Namib's golden sand
Lights up the land.

How can I, but feel bold
Surrounded by the purest gold?
A gentle peace descends upon the sands -
Oh, how I love these desert lands!

Iris Ina Glatz

Legacy

If the Earth was a close friend, you would listen
As she told you of her worries and her fears -
Of people making threats against her future.
You would hold her tightly, telling her
That you loved her and that it would be alright
Then she would be comforted and smile . . .

The sun would come out and the sky would be
As blue as the first cornflowers in summer.
White clouds playing hopscotch
Skimming across the pristine horizon.
You would hear the sweetest birdsong ever
Like straining your ears to catch the singing
From a distant abbey on a hilltop.

Grass would be oh so green underfoot
Like a velvet carpet. The perfume of a
Million flowers hanging heavy in the air
While the gentle humming of bees
Would play ragtag with shimmering butterflies
A soft fragrant breeze gently rustling leaves
On trees - hanging like emerald dewdrops.
As you walk past the silver flowing river
You would stop to drink from the pure, sweet water.

But - if you were the one causing all the worries and fears
You wouldn't care.
The sun would be trying to shine weakly
Through thick, choking, swirling smog
The sky would be a sickly grey colour
Pollution; you were warned
You did not care.

The only noise you would hear then
Would be the dying cries of the sick and hungry
As there would not be enough food to eat
Water, that once was pure and sweet,
Now undrinkable.

The green trees that willingly gave us life
Would now have been sentenced to death
For what?
Just to satisfy Man's utter greed
Birds, bees and butterflies, what were they?
Our children would ask
Too soon we would forget.

So, as the green earth slowly turns brown
And we all gradually die
Pause for a moment in your ravaging of nature
You may hear her sigh

Then as you continue to rape Gaia
For all she possesses
The last thing you will hear
. . . is her silence.

Babsi Sherwin

Soon I Will Be Leaving

New mornings bring no joy for me
In fact the sadness multiplies
For soon I will be leaving here
And each day a part of me just dies

I will leave the trees, the flowers, the fields
Leave the songbirds way on high
No more to see wild beast roam
Or watch fish swim idly by

Leaves shining in the forest
As the rain's soft droplets fall
Or the virgin snow of winter
Will soon be beyond recall

It's with a heavy heart I'm leaving
As my time has nearly come
The competition's almost over
And my final race is run.

Don Woods

My Bonnie Teviotdale

The Scottish Borders

Flowers bloom in the spring
Fields of corn summer brings
Autumn leaves are red and gold
Winter snows with winds so cold
Surrounded by the Cheviot Hills
My Bonnie Teviotdale.

Elizabeth Murray Shipley

Heron

Statuesque and solitary,
Solitude seems to
Suit you
And me.

But my fate
Is joining
That frantic race of life
Just to survive.

You, like grey smoke,
Pulse gracefully
Into space
And disappear.

Heron - stay!
I need your presence
To tell me
Solitude is best.

Lilian Perriman

The Boat Ride

(River Thames - 1992)

Sway water's edge
Lush foam - spits revolving
'Gainst side it halts
Gracefully dissolving.

Bow ever racing
As ship gains momentum
Old Thames, tourists pleases
Such splendour and welcome.

Avoiding the bridge
To turn it manoeuvres
With force of the engine
Coaxing and guiding.

Majestically covered
For deck now revealed.
Full charge - all ahoy!
As boat forces, seething.

Hair brushed by wind
Challenging nature
Damp smell pervades;
Seagulls' adventure.

As home-bound sets sail
Past vessel she misses -
The boat she goes on
Her horn solemnly hisses.

Stephen Shutak

Beyond The Horizon

Wonders of nature never fail
The sky at night - awesome sight
A cold wintry night
As stormclouds gather
And the moon veiled in mystery
Restless as the clouds.
Frosty nights, crisp and bright
'Specially when Jack Frost is about
Wrap up warm, and see his magic
As trees turn to silver
Silhouetting the silvery moon
In all her splendour
But the sunset
By far the best
That golden haze of shimmering light
As the sun sinks down
To take her rest
Just stare in wonder
Sheer delight - peaceful sight
The restless owl would agree
A starry night, romantic and fun
Looking for satellites
Among the stars
Under a bright full moon
Is that Saturn, or is it Mars?
Yes, the sky at night is worth a stare
One wonders, *what is out there?*

Margaret Parnell

Nature's Choice

Have you ever wandered round a wood,
taken in the things that you should:
brought peace of mind to your heart
erased the problems that do start?
Bring freshness to your health,
strengthen the muscles and the core,
breathe in the natural air:
walk with the breeze and the wind
that cleans the nature's soul,
never letting herself dig a hole.
Life growing towards the sun,
not dying without knowing what it's done,
do you need to see what can be achieved
when you're unhappy or aggrieved?
When you lose faith in life we live,
walk amongst the flowers and trees,
you may see what nature can give,
I'm sure it will only please . . .

Gareth Culshaw

Pine Cone

As the lake water ripples,
And the fishes swim beneath,
It sits, insignificantly.
Lacking the beauty of a coral reef,
Or the freedom of the sky,
Yet fully included, as nature passes by.
It cannot move, with the motion of the wind,
Nor join in the chorus when the songbirds sing,
But it exists in happiness,
Dwelling on the notion,
That the pine cone holds nature's secrets
Far bigger than the ocean.

Christian Hinz & Shelley Powell

A Favourite Walk

The bluebells were out early,
Deep blue and white bells too,
Wood anemones, violets,
Where I stopped to admire the view.

This landscape was so beautiful,
It was April, warm and pleasant,
Rabbits scuttling into the hedge,
In the fields, some pheasant.

I loved this favourite bluebell walk,
Climbing up a bit, then down,
It was blissfully quiet and peaceful,
A far cry from the town.

The path led through a stud farm,
The mares stood with their foals,
Some were busy feeding,
Some frolicked; such sweet souls.

Then back into the bluebell wood,
And pretty gardens passing by,
With tulips and forsythia,
And the nodding Pheasant Eye.

My walk finished at the church,
Some boys were climbing trees,
There were butterflies and robins,
And a couple of bumblebees.

I stood and leant against the fence,
Beauty - I could not but stare,
I absorbed the green fields, the golden rape,
I breathed in deep the country air.

June Melbourn

Controversy Over Weather

Why do we talk about weather?
Do we really give a toss?
Can we change it? No, of course not,
Someone's gain is our loss.

We carry on when it's raining,
We moan when the sun don't shine,
And when it shines
It's far too hot for me and mine.

Now what happens when it's snowing?
When there's sleet or piles of snow,
We go indoors, and start to moan
And say 'I know where that lot can go'.

We want good weather for weddings,
For funerals and christenings too,
But we all want snow for Christmas,
It's hard trying to please me and you.

And when we go on vacation
By gum if the sun don't shine,
The kids all scream and Mum gets cross
And Dad will get a hard time.

If I ever get to Heaven
I want to be put in charge
Of weather all round the world,
I don't think the task's too large.

What a wonderful job this could be,
Sun all day and rain by night,
And always a lukewarm sea,
Well we can dream, can't we?

Hazel Palmer

The Water Element

Nature's living element,
Water in its liquid state.
Rain, rain, rain, falling from the sky.
Streams, streams, streams, running on the ground.
Waves, waves, waves, swelling from oceans.
Feel the sheer power of moving water!
Water has a changing mood.

Nature's living element,
Water in its solid state.
Hail, hail, hail, falling from the sky.
Snow, snow, snow, covering the ground.
Ice, ice, ice, cracking from glaciers.
Feel the bitterness of freezing water!
Water has a changing mood.

Nature's living element,
Water in its gaseous state.
Clouds, clouds, clouds, forming in the sky.
Fog, fog, fog, hovering above ground.
Steam, steam, steam, jetting from geysers.
Feel the hot temper of boiling water!
Water has a changing mood.

Eunice Ogunkoya

The Fenland Revisited

I am here once more, alone among the marshes,
Listening to the squelching of the mud,
The faint splashing of playful voles,
The croaking of the frogs,
The honking geese: all disturbing
The keen early morning air,
That turned reeds into hissing snakes.

I watched a time-honoured dawn,
Draw back the curtain of night,
And send a bolt of dazzling gold
Earthwards, to show reflections of stars
On the surface of the lake.

Wraith-like spirals of mist,
Haunted and deluded reality,
Brought spirits of ancient tribes,
Rising from the sediment of history,
To rule a land that was rightfully theirs.

I felt the past mingle with the present,
And was privileged to be acquainted
With the coming future of the Fens.

Raymond W Seaton

A Change Is Required

Walking through the woods in springtime
Wild flowers can be seen blooming everywhere
My mind is filled with the marvellous signs of nature
And my lungs are filled with the wonderful fresh air.

I see the green buds bursting on the trees
Blossoms appearing on buds that were forlorn
Blackbirds scratching in the earth in search of earthworms
All signs that nature has been reborn.

It is the time of the year that I love most
Knowing the warmth of the sun will drive the winter chills away
Every year the spring appears earlier than before
Which is not a good thing, or so they say.

For it is a potent reminder that things are changing
That the Earth is getting warmer year by year
That the way we live is causing global warming
And that a future catastrophe is something we should fear.

The consequences will be that the ice caps will melt
Causing the sea levels to rise everywhere
That the low-lying areas will be submerged
That we must act quickly is now very clear.

This calls for a dramatic change in our lifestyle
And that sacrifices are something we must make
It's no good doing nothing, hoping everything will be well
Action is required now for everyone's sake.

Ron Martin

Bluebell Woods

The woods were quite close to where we lived
When I was young, in the South Wales valley.
The mountains loomed just beyond the houses
Fern-clad, they were our ideal playground.

Once clear of the last house, the road rises
Steeply to enter the narrow lanes
Bordered by hedges they wind forever
Twisting, climbing, to the mountain's top.

Hedges with wild roses, honeysuckle
Hawthorn blossom, hazel, elderberry
Not far along the lane, across a field
Is a lovely wood, a favourite one.

The trees are tall and straight searching for light
Whilst on the ground they are surrounded
By a carpet, a sea of bobbing blooms
Thousands upon thousands of bluebells.

In the spring we children gathered armfuls
To take to Mother, to brighten the day
Though they did not have a lovely aroma
They made up for this with their beauty.

Even today in later years I revisit
The lanes and see again the bluebell woods
They still exist there and delight the eye
A timeless and everlasting gift.

Terry Daley

Nature

Every creature great and small
From the beast down to the bee,
From the flower up to the tree so tall
Are nature's family.

Go out into the country
Breathe refreshing air
There's wonderment in plenty
For all of us to share.

For every newborn animal
What joy it is to see
And wonder at the miracle
Little lamb - who made thee?

The perfumes and the colours
No human hand can make
Or imitate the contours
But only try - and fake.

And who are we to put to the test
The wonders of the world
For Mother Nature's way is best
Her banners are unfurled.

Betty Prescott

The Magic Of The Garden

Looking out of the window
Such beauty do I see.
Torrential rain beats hard
Against the windowpanes.
As I listen to the whistling wind
There's magic in the garden,
Grey and black clouds above.
Neatly mowed is the well-shaped lawn.
Tidy are the flower beds.
Flowers in gay-coloured dresses,
Their heads tossing back and fro.
Blown always by the force of the wind.
Delicately their perfume fills the air.
So peaceful and serene.
Stop to look around the garden
For there's magic in the air.
Planned to perfection by an artist's gardener.
Such a labour of love he's shared.
Yet! only God has made it all worthwhile
And shown you all His love.
In the beauty of your garden
His gift to you from above.

Doreen Petherick Cox

Songs Men Sing

Many are the songs men sing
Of purple heather, mossy ring;
Of springing turf and bells of blue,
Of Scotland and their love so true.

No Scotsman I, yet my voice too
Is raised in wonder. Praise unto
Whomsoever created you!
What seeing eye, creative hand
Carved out these rocks and hills so grand?

This beauty glowers, grim and stark.
An awesome power has made this mark.
The mountain pass through granite rock
Doth human strength and Man's pride mock.

My homeland's hills are green and fair,
The streams are gentle, silver, slow.
The fields are gold with corn, and there
The skylark sings and poppies show.

In early summer, beech is queen
And southern hills are clothed with green.
An emerald-green so fresh and bright
The eyes rejoice, the heart is light.

But men of the plain, the valley, the fen,
All sing their songs and wonder when
Other men sing their hymns of praise
To that great Pow'r whose works amaze.

O human hands, whose puny skill
Is yet so small and mortal still,
Clasp Thou in prayer that eyes may see
All beauty created here for Thee.

Deirdre White

The Amazon Aunt

She rides her golden Palomino like an Amazon,
Her brown hands tangled in his creamy mane,
Her lined hawk face leans down to his neck;
His ears, his eyes roll back for her signs.
They sway together, breathe together,
Deep chests fill and strong ribs splay,
Like tango dancers they move away,
Barely touching the earth in flight.
Down to earth once more she assumes human form,
Cooks up food on the old wood stove for her brood,
Her ravenous waiting horde. Strides out to hurl curses
At a circling hawk in a staccato African tongue,
Takes a gun from the rack on the wall to shoot,
Or to shake at his fleet shadow. She loves us all like a lioness,
Impartial and fair to motherless me, and her own,
And her only rule is kindness to the animals,
Those who are dumb and cannot speak. At nights
She winds the old gramophone, drops on it a heavy disc
With a rich thud, then the thick needle, and we wait
For the brassy faraway ballroom sounds
To creak out onto the sultry air. And then she takes us
Into her arms one by one: her heifers, she calls us,
Holds us firmly to her, one arm out and we dance,
Skinny legs round the room to a schmaltzy waltz,
An alien sound on an African night,
Until we collapse weak and laughing on the floor.

Liz Davies

Waiting

Over the fields the mists are hanging
The sky is grey and so forbidding
Trees just standing with branches bare,
Nothing of interest to see or stare
Patches of snow frozen on grass
Cars throw up slush as they pass
Workers go home with hooded heads
No stopping to chat, a quick 'hi' instead
Children trying to see through frosted glass
See only vague shapes as they pass
The afternoon's gone, it's dark already
Can't see a thing, steady! Steady!
Nature's holding her curtain down
While the grey shrub, frosted, turns brown
The temperature drops, heating rises
But wait! Soon there'll be surprises
First we'll notice the nights are shorter
And yes! The tips of bulbs in the border
Darling little snowdrops peeping up in lawn
It will be warmer with each dawn
So grin and bear this winter waiting
O glorious spring! We're waiting! Waiting!

Millicent Blanche Colwell

The Miracle Of Snowdrops

One cold and frosty evening
when the ground was bleak and bare,
as I wandered through my garden
there were no flowers anywhere.
Well it blew and it snowed
all through the night.
Then early next morning
I saw this beautiful sight.
The weak sun was shining
on that January day
as pale green shoots
of snowdrops
were making their way,
thrusting up through snow and ice
it was a picture to behold.
While everyone was sleeping,
in the night that was so cold
had the fairy folk been busy
as they had just appeared
or was it one of God's miracles
that happens every year?

Doreen E Hampshire

Hillmorton

As we walk the canals of Hillmorton
We see some lovely sights
Swans are gently gliding by
Or mother duck with her brood behind
Dragonflies of lovely hues hover on plants
Gaily painted barges going through the locks
Some with dogs on board
Decorated buckets filled with flowers
And people lying on barges catching the sun
We walk under a bridge and find a sunny spot
Sit having our lunch as the world goes by
Across in the field we see the wild rabbits
Running for cover as a train goes by
There are sheep grazing in a field
And cows in another
We walk along the lane to home
On the way passing horses in the fields
And birds singing in the trees
Thinking this area of Rugby is a lovely place.

Diana Daley

Sweet Song Of Spring

All on a February morning,
Dark, and sleeping still,
Upon the air, from Heaven it seems,
A blackbird's beauteous trill,

He sings, his heart so joyous,
His love of life to tell,
His music comes from God above,
Our hearts with love to fill,

No human voice, no violin
Can replicate the sound,
The notes that come from blackbird's song
Have never yet been found,

He sings to us of a new day,
Of promise as spring unfolds,
His song so pure, so perfect,
Has never been sweeter told.

Dorothy M Mitchell

Seascape

The crashing ocean's tide smashes against the jagged rocky shore,
Reaching its destination and progressing no more,
The sea currents creating chaos on the ocean floor,
The sea a blazing pool of activity to the core.

When the river to the ocean goes
Nothing to hinder its progress shows,
The meeting marked by mighty blows.
The climax to the clash of the bellicose.

The rough-textured open sea,
Hides a power which is manifest to see,
The brilliant sunlight mirrors against the ocean,
The bright light changing with the sun and sea's motion.

From heaving seas reaching a crescendo,
To rivers and streams in gentle flow.
From contrast to contrast the water runs its course,
Depositing small rivulets, brooks, creeks gently, in place of force.

The captured water in the rock pool placidly sits,
With a variety of creepy-crawlies in its midst,
An end which barely befits,
A beginning marked by a mighty blitz.

Hasan Erdogan

Promise Of Spring

There is a faint, sweet
Stirring of spring in the
Air today,
That intoxicates my senses.
Nature seems to have
Shrugged off her
Winter coat as the
Watery sun
Hangs low in the sky,
Barely warms the pale
Green buds into
New life,
And the cold, dark earth
Brings forth a
Multitude of shoots of
Hyacinth and daffodils.
A flock of wild geese
Fly in perfect symmetry in the
Brilliant winter sky,
Exploding in a riot of sound.
My restless heart
Stirs with the promise of spring,
The miracle that nature will bring.

Elizabeth Doroszkiewicz

Getting Away With Murder?

She screamed in: as her hurricane-forced friends,
partnered a torrential downpour from the west.
Roaring ferociously like an angry wounded lion.

Whipping, beating up, the relentless demon waves
of the unforgiving River Mersey,
into an eerie, haunting, salty, mystical mist.

Racing hard against the turbulent Irish Sea.
Speeding violently and uncontrollably,
like a frenzied tropical cyclone.

Ripping tearing timbers, twisting ornamental structured iron,
snapping, splitting, strong well-established trees,
with just the fearsome waves of her hands.

Leaving a catalogue of cruel catastrophes;
death, disaster, fear and mayhem in her wake.
Fortunately; I lived to survive yet another one of
                              Mother Nature's storms.

Tommy McBride

Untitled

It was a cold, lonely night
Out on the dark hillside.
Silhouetted against a dim moon
Stood the skeletal figures of the
Forest's spiny, scattered trees.
A badger silently burrowed about,
His white stripe barely visible in
The gloomy night. The only sound
Was an occasional rustle as the
Night creatures stirred the leaves and branches.
A mouse gently nosed its way out
And peered cautiously around, sniffing,
Twitching. Sensing no immediate danger
He edged his wriggling way through the sparse
Undergrowth. The badger ignored this tiny
Dim-witted intruder as it searched for
Food. Above, however, on a silent wingspan
Encompassing all its prey, flew in the supposed
Wise owl. Its eyes bored downwards.

Ann McLeod

Sweet Daffodil Song

Hey! Spring from the gloom,
daffodils are in bloom,
yellow is everywhere.
Colour is blazing,
you are amazing,
I just stand and stare.

You are inspiring,
I am admiring,
beauty on the air.
To the sky you're aspiring,
one glance I'm desiring,
brightness on the bare.

Dancing, swaying,
with hush you are saying,
come look at me.
Willing, I follow,
how can there be sorrow
as spring paints glory?

In the fields, hedgerows,
wild and free you glow,
yellow is everywhere.
Colour is blazing,
you are amazing,
I just stand and stare.

Oh sweet daffodil,
down lane and up hill,
stately, serene,
gracious with green,
making hazy sheen,
by sparkling stream,
I love you.

Hey! Spring from the gloom,
daffodils are in bloom,
yellow is everywhere.
How could I be sad?
You make me so glad,
I just stand and stare.

Carol Ann Darling

Passing Seasons

The path is dry - dusty;
without life-giving rain.
Branches hang low,
leaves listless.
Blossom falls,
lighter than feathers
through the still, hot air -
laying a carpet before my feet.

I smile . . . the first in months . . .
for the pink and white
of April's flowers
remind me of you, my love.

The petals of your life,
one by one, fell away . . .
their season ended.
Your summers spent . . .
you were no more;
yet the essence of you
like sweet perfume,
lingers on.

At this moment,
in this place,
I feel you touch my heart . . .
melt winter's ice.

Pat Spear

Autumn Leaves

Autumn leaves, fascinating work of nature
Palette impossible to replicate, merging
Soft colours too subtle to discriminate, yet
God might permit Man the hand of nature to appreciate.
As a nature-lover to instinctively discover during
Fall, it is a glimpse of Heaven's hall
Leaves once green, red and brown, tumble down
Transformed into nature's crown, while summer flowers are fully
Blown; then for a moment Man is by tristesse seized,
Only to be spared and by the variety of shapes and sizes eased
Indented, spear-edged, serrated, quincunx and curvilinear
No world genius could have invented, hence
Discontented, to all his gods for shades that
Skill indented, but can never emulate the
Dame who is an old hand, superb at her game.
Ringing new changes on the old and familiar.
This poet scarce knows where to start faced
With nature's works of art, which become a warm part
Of his heart. Her many môdes matching his divers moods.
See an uncanny image of a Zulu shield, a small leaf
Whose colour and white striped pattern recalling
The spilling of crimson British blood, released by
A short stabbing assegai, in darkest Africa of days gone by.
Now might catch the eye of an artist passing by, who
Collecting them, on to a lampshade fastens them
Then in a drawing room, dispels the gloom,
By a constant autumn glow.
Those leaves form a coat of many colours, with
A tinge of sorrow, brings today a bright now and tomorrow.

Graham Watkins

Nature's Paradise - New Zealand

I know a place that's full of trees.
Of native birds and roaring seas.
A place with over 50 shades of green.
Of culture, history and places unseen.
A terrain of altitude, and snowy peaks.
Acres of bush land with bubbling creeks.
Of waterfalls, lakes and beaches with sand.
Parks full of geysers shooting out from the land.
Farmland with livestock and produce for us.
Cities that hustle and bustle and fuss.
Volcanoes and mountains create 'Middle Earth'
Plains full of Tussock give movies their worth!
Remarkable sunrises and sunsets each day.
Picturesque scenery takes your breath away.
Creatures unique, some big and some small
Fancy a coffee, then go to the mall!
A country of competitiveness, they love the outdoors.
Of compassion and charity, they help for a cause.
Endless hot summers to soak up a tan.
Winter for snow sports, if you're a fan.
I know of a place that lives and breathes.
A photographer's Utopia of all culture and creeds.
Of towns and villages where people stop and smile.
But don't take my word, come and stay for a while.
I could talk on forever sharing the wealth,
But the best thing is to come and judge for yourself.
This country full of beauty will make you look twice.
This place is New Zealand, and nature's paradise.

Helen Moll

God's Tapestry Of Love

A feast before my very eyes.
This piece of Heaven leads me into paradise,
and, mesmerised by golden fields,
I taste the richness of the fruit they yield.

Bright sunny days and moonlit nights
illuminate the ancient olive trees.
For as they shiver in the gently breeze,
they dazzle me with green and silver lights.

As autumn limps its way ahead,
the mauves and blues of lavender are gone.
Replaced by hues of browns and reds;
the glowing embers of a setting sun.

I've glimpsed a look through Heaven's door,
and seen what it may have in store.
An arc of vibrant colours rich with gold.
God's tapestry of love unfolds.

So I let creation minister to me,
through every flower, leaf and tree and see
a multitude of stitches, fashioned by my Father's hands.
Each one a precious gift to all mankind.

Elizabeth Mason

The Tree

In glorious green mantle you enhance this bright day
Oh! Tree so divine - stay forever this way
From tender young shoot now maturity - so lends
Firm branches rich laden in green splendour transcends
Outstretched in sheer pleasure - each bough doth proclaim
'A sight to behold' forever its aim.

Enjoy this sweet summer Oh! Tree of good grace
While nature's soft touch you so fondly embrace
Come autumn thy season of warm richest light
Each colour triumphant - in murmured delight
As tender leaves wither- then to earth gently fall
Forever this story - now surely recall.

'Life - has beginning - but life has no end'
'Mother Earth's' greatest wisdom does surely portend
As chill winter approaches - in place now to reign
No sadness descends on this tree's vast domain

All now await spring's soft delicate touch
Deep vigil quite silent - yet! Secure in so much
Life's constant return a promise so made
In nature's sweet breath 'life' never shall fade
Each moment of beauty so transient in time
Speaks forever 'renewal' in fondness sublime.

Henrietta Valmore

Calendar

January brings jewels of ice
To sparkle under city skies.
February brings the frosty wind
Until the colder days rescind.
March brings dancing pearls of rain
To make the gardens new again.
April brings a swoop of sparrows
Flocking around streets so narrow.
May brings a once more brighter day
And the sun to warm the woodland way.
June brings flowers of crimson and gold
To give pleasure to young and old.
July brings a blue sky lullaby
To soothe away the baby's cry.
August brings a cloth so fine
On which to place the summer wine.
September brings autumn's colour
And trees like kings in all their splendour.
October brings the hail and gale
The sweet fresh taste of home-made ale.
In November leaves of amber
Fall on path of country rambler.
December brings the year's end in
Ready for new life and light to begin.

Nigel Evans

The Law Of The Sea

Foam as white as
freshly laundered cloth
blows to shore when
storm-whipped waves smash
across the shallow bar.

'Power the motor,'
the fishermen yell.
'Power the motor
against the swell.
Power the motor,'
is their death knell.

Then pounding waves
lift, spin
and crash
the innocent
who venture in
light boats
to run the tide . . .

Foam-laundered cloth
is now
their shroud.

Leigh Vickridge

Forward Press Information

We hope you have enjoyed reading this book - and that you will continue to enjoy it in the coming years.

If you like reading and writing poetry drop us a line, or give us a call, and we'll send you a free information pack.

Alternatively if you would like to order further copies of this book or any of our other titles, then please give us a call or log onto our website at
www.forwardpress.co.uk

**Forward Press Ltd. Information
Remus House
Coltsfoot Drive
Peterborough
PE2 9JX**

(01733) 898101